MIDNIGHT MARQUEE
Number 76

Editors
Gary J. Svehla
Susan Svehla

Graphic Design Interior
Gary J. Svehla

Cover Design
Title Page Design
Gary J. Svehla

Copy Editor
Susan Svehla

Contributing Writers
Anthony Ambrogio; Mark Clark;
Daniel J. Graffeo; Mark Allan Gunnells;
Jonathan Malcolm Lampley;
Arthur Lundquist; Carl Schultz;
Bryan Senn; Brian Smith;
Cindy Collins Smith; Gary J. Svehla;
Steven Thornton; Neil Vokes

Acknowledgments
Aaron Christensen; Warner Home Video;
Fox Home Video; Universal Home Video;
Bender Helper Publicity;
Scott Essman

Illustrator
Allen K. Koszowski

Publisher
Midnight Marquee Press, Inc.

Midnight Marquee
Number 76
February 2009
Copyright 2009© by Gary J. Svehla

Published irregularly for $10 per issue by Midnight Marquee Press, Inc.

Articles and art should be transmitted electonically and will remain the property of the writer/artist and copyright holder, who will retain the rights. If material intended for publication is sent to us via regular mail, it is the sender's responsibility to include return postage. No responsibility is taken for unsolicited material.

Editorial views expressed by writers are not necessarily those of the publisher, Midnight Marquee Press. Nothing from the digital on-line magazine or the print edition may be reproduced or shared in any media without the expressed written permission of the publisher. The Midnight Marquee Press offices are located at: 9721 Britinay Lane, Parkville, MD 21234; website: http://www.midmar.com; e-mail: midmargary@aol.com

Letters of comment addressed to Midnight Marquee or Susan and Gary Svehla will be considered for publication unless the writer requests otherwise.

Letters of comment are encouraged; please send all comments to midmargary@aol.com and label your comments "Comments for issue #76."

We are always looking for writers to submit articles. Please discuss any article suggestions first with Gary J. Svehla at midmargary@aol.com and check the Style Sheet link on our website to get ideas for style and formatting. Length of articles may vary. We take them long and short. But remember, our emphasis is mainly on the classic horror and science ficiton movies of the Golden Age, but our definition of classic and Golden Age is not based upon specific decades or year of production necessarily, but upon the artistic content that reflects the heart and style of early horror cinema.

Copies are mailed, within the USA, for the cost of the issue plus $5 Priority Mail or $3 for the slower Media Mail. Issues are sent in sturdy mailers and are cardboard reinforced, so they should arrive at your home in near mint condition. Foreign orders are welcome, but shipping costs vary. Check with us.

TABLE OF CONTENTS

3   **Marquee Mutterings: Editorial**
by Gary J. Svehla

5   **Forum/Against 'Em: Psycho... Most Influential Modern Horror Movie?**
Edited by Anthony Ambrogio

38   **Halloween: Slicing and Dicing the Urban Legend**
by Daniel J. Graffeo

50   **Jamie Lee Curtis and The Virginity Myth**
by Mark Allan Gunnells

60   **Plan 9 From Outer Space: Why the Plan Works**
by Carl Schultz

64   **DVD Reviews**
by Gary J. Svehla

119   **Grave Diggings [Letters]**

Welcome to the digital premiere of *Midnight Marquee*, now in its 76th issue and 45th year of publication. Think of how technology has changed our magazine throughout the decades. Debuting in the summer of 1963, when I had just turned 13, it was then called *Gore Creatures*. The first issue was reproduced using hectograph gelatin pads (a few copies were typed using carbon paper and one or two were even hand written). We evolved soon into ditto or spirit duplication, and then mimeo. Testing the offset printing waters, we produced several issues that were half-mimeo and half-offset. Soon we went to an all offset format, laying out each issue using cut-and-paste layouts on oversized boards. Then the electronic typewriter with multiple fonts became available, and at home typesetting became a reality. And then the 64k Kaypro arrived, this early computer unfortunately did not allow us to design the entire magazine within the computer, but the text could be shifted, edited, resized and reformatted. Soon we committed to our lifelong love affair with the Apple Macintosh and at last the entire magazine could be created on the computer using publication software such as PageMaker and now InDesign. The magazine continued to evolve and change throughout the decades.

But perhaps our biggest transcending action has been the evolution from hard copy print magazine to a magazine produced digitally online. And even though this is our 76th issue, it is the first to be produced in this new way. No hard copy version exists, unless a reader prints out the contents of the issue using his or her own printer at home or at work. And this is our first issue of the magazine in full color.

Some collectors barely read (shame on them!) the contents of the magazines they faithfully collect, for their thing is the "bag and board" aspect of buying film magazines. Maintaining their treasures in pristine near mint condition means avoiding touching, reading and flipping through the magazine pages. The major goal of such collectors is to keep the magazine sealed and protected from human fingerprints and environmental factors (UV rays, acid rain). Our digital evolution will no doubt affect these collectors the most.

Other collectors love the tactile experience of smelling fresh printers' inks and turning back a cover for the very first time. The simple touch of

Gary and Buddy take a break from mag work to prepare for the football playoffs. Unfortunately, the Ravens lost to the&^#*&%^& Steelers.

Issue 76

flipping through magazine pages and feeling each and every page, studying every photo or piece of art, reading the text and enjoying all the letters, articles and even the editorial, becomes the ultimate experience. For my generation, this became a ritual cemented in our childhood and one that follows us through life.

Until now.

Digital reproduction means we sit at our computer and gawk at the monitor and enjoy the magazine online. We can no longer touch the pages, smell printer's ink or bag and board the final product. We can download the PDF file and save it in a *Midnight Marquee* desk folder. We can even print it out at home and perhaps go to the local photocopying store to have the issue bound. So in a sense, the hard copy print out still exists for people who demand such permanence. But the bottom line is that readers of our magazine will have to learn to enjoy it in a new way.

What excites me is that many people who never heard of *Midnight Marquee* or never saw a copy might finally be exposed to a magazine that has continued to celebrate the world of classic horror movies since 1963. To all those fresh new eyes, welcome. Enjoy! Send your letters of comment (hopefully, we will publish them). And to those loyal subscribers and followers of the magazine, welcome back and recharge. Keep those letters of comment coming as well!

The new look *Midnight Marquee* uses color reproduction to a much greater extent, and even when writing about black-and-white horror film classics, color graphics may be introduced by way of photographs, lobby cards, posters, pressbooks and other colorful promotions created to promote black-and-white movies. For our reviews, DVD covers can now be reproduced in color. Our layout can evolve and grow more ambitious. The only limits are no longer financial but only the limits of our imagination.

Hopefully, in our new digital domain, we will be able to publish more frequently *Midnight Marquee* and our companion magazine, *Mad About Movies,* and hopefully revive *Movie Mystique*. Keep checking our website for announcements of new issue availability. And between issues, enjoy our *Midnight Marquee/Gary J. Svehla Blog* that can also be accessed via our website (http://www.midmar.com). Also, Sue has redesigned our web site making it more informative and user friendly.

Please remember just how important your feedback becomes. *Midnight Marquee* will only improve if readers respond to each new issue by writing us at midmargary@aol.com. All suggestions, ideas, criticisms, praise—anything. We are always looking for new staff writers and articles that would interest readers of either magazine.

The new adventure begins, and hopefully, *Midnight Marquee* won't be seen as run of the mill. We believe that our insight, passion and innovations will demonstrate why the magazine has survived for 45 years. We believe the best is yet to come.

BACK TO PRINT: 2/9/09

After this all digital issue appeared last September, readers, many of whom were not computer literate, pleaded for us to revisit the idea of publishing a hard copy magazine. The Classic Horror Film Board was front and center in this plea, so due to the opportunity given us by Book Surge at Amazon.com, the hard print version has returned. We'll keep putting the issue up online free, but for our diehard fans, a professionally printed mag can be ordered for $10 plus $4 shipping.

PSYCHO FORUM/ AGAINST 'EM

Edited by Anthony Ambrogio

Most Influential Modern Horror Movie?

There's nothing like a good debate to get the juices flowing. And Gary J. Svehla knows how to spark more debates than all the 2008 presidential candidates put together. Most recently, he compiled a controversial list of the 13 most influential horror movies: *Frankenstein* (1931), *King Kong* (1933), *The Black Cat* (1934), *Cat People* (1942), *Frankenstein Meets the Wolf Man* (1943), *The Thing* (1951), *I Was a Teenage Werewolf* (1956), *Horror of Dracula* (1958), *Black Sunday* (1960), *Night of the Living Dead* (1968), *The Exorcist* (1973), *Halloween* (1978) and *Ringu* (1998).

This list sparked several debates at once. The longest had to do with a particularly glaring (to some) omission. First, contributor Mark Clark crossed swords with Gary, followed by Brian Smith, Arthur Lundquist and Steven Thornton. Bryan Senn was on hand to cheer on the troops; Anthony Ambrogio did his diplomatic best to straddle all fences; and Jonathan Malcolm Lampley, Neil Vokes and Cindy Collins Smith all added their 10 cents' worth. (That's two cents' worth, adjusted for inflation).

Who won? That's for you, the reader, to decide...

Mark: I was completely baffled when Gary left *Psycho* (1960) off his list of "Groundbreakers: The 13 Most Influential Horror Films" (*Midnight Marquee* 75 [2006], pp. 5-15). I mean, it's one of the most influential films in the history of movies, period. Then I figured that the only possible explanation was that Gary considered it a "thriller" but not a horror film, although I would have considered Gary far too bright to fall for that old canard. The way I see it, *Psycho* is not only a horror film but also one of the quintessential modern Gothics—an archetype.

Gary: Mark, *Psycho* is definitely a horror film, and I always considered it one. The film made my short list of the 13 most influential horror movies, but I cut it for a very sound reason.

As I defined in my introduction, an influential film is one that shaped or determined many other films that followed in its wake. Influential movies are not necessarily great or archetypal, but they do create a sub-genre or a new way of doing horror that many others follow.

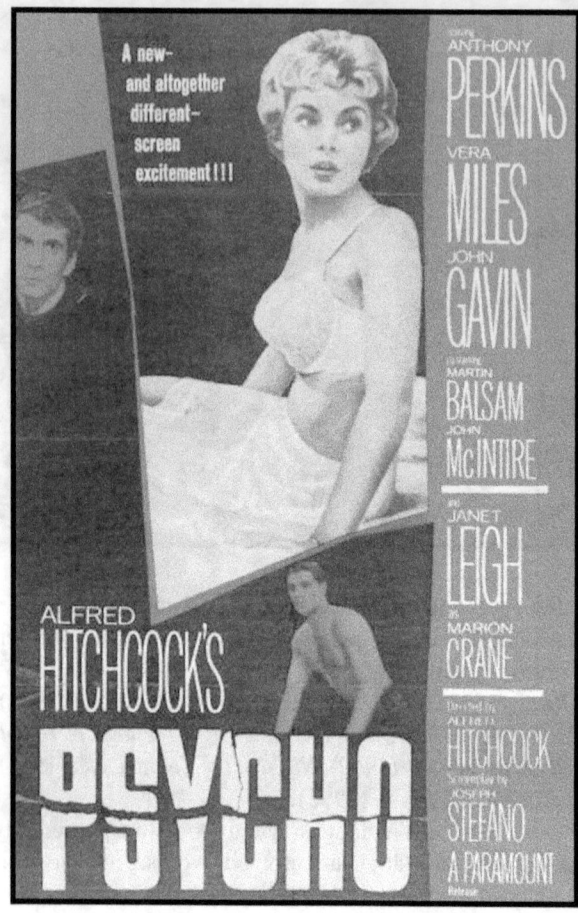

Psycho—what sub-genre or movies did it inspire? Perhaps Amicus and Hammer's psychologically based horror films (almost all of them so vastly inferior that any influence is overshadowed by their artistic failings).

I see *Psycho* as a singular film experience, one that stands alone as a classic. What Hitchcock achieved is on a level so much higher than the best of the psycho films that followed. Even films such as *Scream of Fear* (aka *Taste of Fear* [1961]) and *Paranoiac* (1963) pale by comparison. These movies (and all the other inferior ones) simply copied the idea of the unidentified psycho who is revealed at the very end, but not much else.

Arthur: Gary, "*Psycho*... what sub-genre or movies did it inspire?" How about the entire oeuvre of Brian De Palma?

Gary Arthur, come on. That's not correct! *Vertigo* (1958), *Rear Window* (1954) and any other number of Hitchcock films inspired De Palma, not *just Psycho*. True, *Psycho*'s influence is there...but De Palma was most inspired by the entire body of Hitchcock's work and not *Psycho* alone!

Arthur: Okay, let's talk about specific De Palma *Psycho* knockoffs. Killings in *Sisters* (1973) and *Carrie* (1976) use *Psycho* death-music. *Phantom of the Paradise* (1974) and *Body Double* (1984) re-do the shower scene, as does *Dressed to Kill* (1980)—with a shower scene and an elevator-as-"shower-stall" scene. Hell, *Dressed to Kill* is practically a *Psycho* remake, from killing off the main character to cross-dressing killers to the psychologist's explanation at the end.

Most importantly, no Hitchcock film is as ruthless in making us care for a main character and then heartlessly killing him/her off, as *Psycho*. That approach ties together *Phantom of the Paradise*, *Carrie*, *The Fury* (1978), *Dressed to Kill*, *Body Double*, etc. Indeed, it is practically the man's modus operandi.

Gary: Yes, the man's entire early career was one long love fest with Hitchcock, and *Psycho* was at the forefront. You mention *Sisters*, *Dressed to Kill*, etc. But is paying homage (and *Obsession* [1976] is to *Vertigo* as *Sisters* is to *Psycho*) the same thing as being influential? I can see people defining it both ways.

Arthur: I would not define all those moments "homages." By the time of *Dressed to Kill*, I think they become downright plagiarism.

Mark: Let me piggyback on Arthur's comments and count the ways that *Psycho* inspired *several* sub-genres. First of all, it kicked off a whole raft of pseudo-*Psycho* thrillers, not only including the long string of Hammer black-and-white thrillers from *Scream of Fear* on but also sundry other knockoffs like *Homicidal* (1961) and the 1962 *Caligari*. This wave of psychological thrillers led to *What Ever Happened to Baby Jane?* (1962), and that in turn kicked off the whole Horror Hag sub-genre.

Gary: Mark, you create a very liberal line of influences. I take total exception with the Southern Gothics, the so-called Horror Hag movies. I think that *What Ever Happened to Baby Jane?* spawned movies such as *Hush, Hush, Sweet Charlotte* (1964) and the rest. I don't see *Psycho* influencing them (although there is blade imagery in *Charlotte*). I see them as movies that attempted to revitalize the fading careers of formerly classy Hollywood female stars. The only influence from *Psycho* that matters here is the image of the mummified face of Norman Bates' mother. Think Joan Crawford!

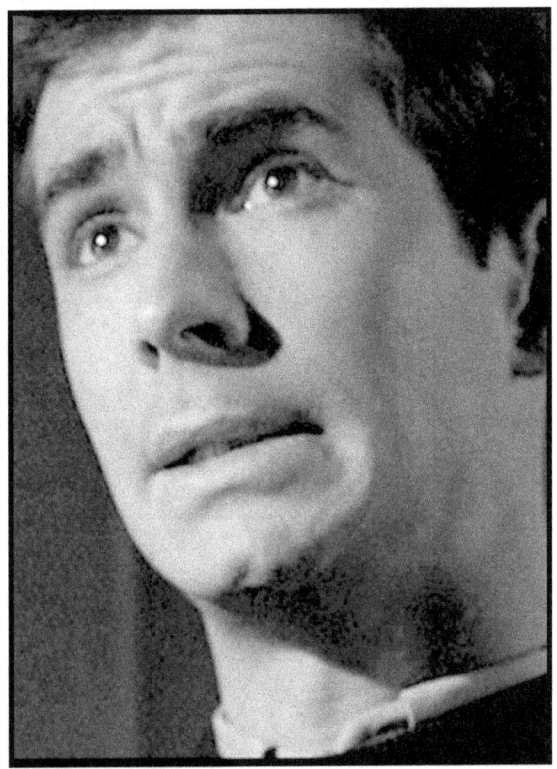

Anthony Perkins as the tormented Norman Bates

Mark: *Psycho* was an even more widely influential overseas. Its echoes can be heard in scores of Euro thrillers. The Italian *gialli* would probably never have emerged if *Psycho* hadn't paved the way.

Gary: Good point, especially as it applies to Dario Argento's early movies. But were the *gialli* influenced by *Psycho* or by Hitchcock's entire oeuvre? True, many of these films feature fiends with blades and walking wounded with deep psychological scars. *Psycho* influenced them, of course—but so did *Rear Window*, *Vertigo* and other Hitchcock visions.

Mark: And the American slasher film wouldn't have taken shape without the *gialli* (and *Psycho*) as forerunners. Not to mention the raft of Hitchcockian thrillers that have aped *Psycho* over the years. Or here's another measure: How many horror films feature young women murdered while bathing?

Gary: Mark, are you suggesting that *every* movie made after 1960 featuring a fiend wielding a knife was "influenced" by *Psycho*? My heavens, the Val Lewton production

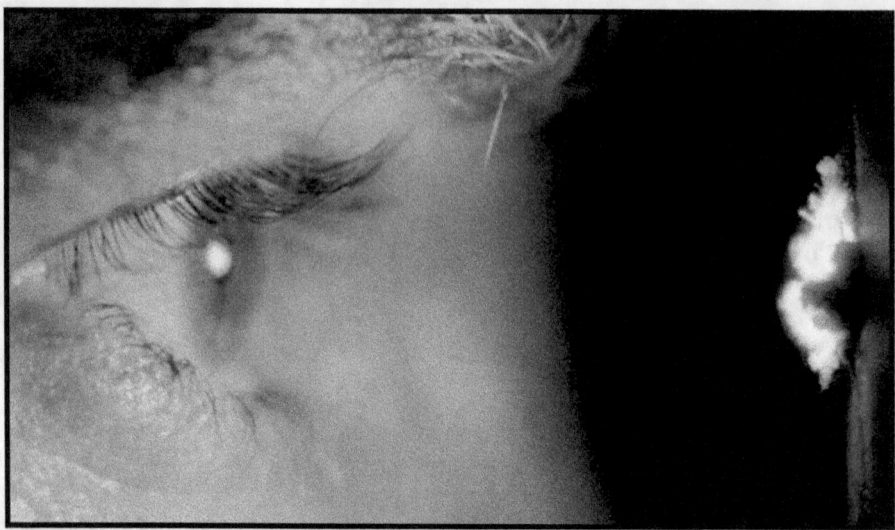

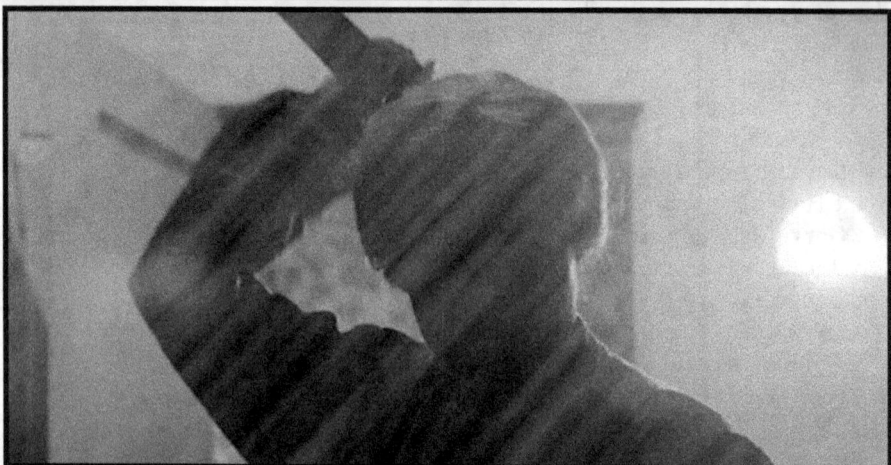

Top: Norman, always the voyeur, eyeballs the room rented by Marion Crane; Bottom: Norman, dressed as Mother, prepares to slaughter Marion Crane as she showers.

The Seventh Victim (1943) features a woman terrified and threatened in the shower, a sequence that many argue influenced the similar sequence in *Psycho*. And a shadowy fiend pursues the heroine with a knife, as he waits hiding in the shadows. The imagery of the naked nubile female, vulnerable and alone in the bath, comes directly from Victorian literature and lives on, especially, in the movies. What Hitchcock added to the mix was the phallic knife. But is every twisted fiend with a blade "influenced" by Norman Bates? Many film noir entries feature psychopaths armed with knives, and I believe these films influenced the *gialli* genre as much as the horror movies did. In fact, by definition, the *giallo* genre is more thriller than horror. That image of the knife as weapon does not solely arrive from the horror film genre. Certainly, night stalkers with long knives populated movies long before *Psycho*. That wasn't a Hitchcock invention, and Hitch himself even used that imagery well before *Psycho*. (I'm thinking of Reggie Nalder in *The Man Who Knew Too Much* [1956]).

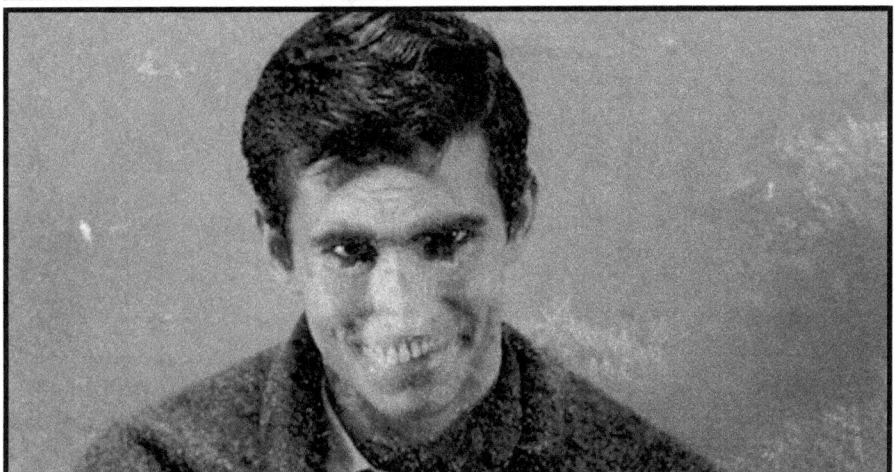

At the film's conclusion, the insane Norman Bates merges with the image of his decaying mother.

Brian: Of course, earlier movies featured psycho killers—most notably *M* (1931), with Peter Lorre. But psycho killers became a 1960s-1970s movie staple, eventually branching off into the 1980s slasher films.

Mark: If you look at the modern horror film and trace it from the leaves back to the root, that root is *Psycho*.

Steven: Agreed. There are still echoes of traditional, Universal-style horror throughout 1960s' horror cinema, but you also begin to see a depiction of human evil that is less fanciful and considerably darker than anything on display in a traditional monster movie.

Psycho is surely the starting point for this.

Gary: Surely? I think that James Bell's performance (as Dr. Galbraith) in Jacques Tourneur's *The Leopard Man* (1943) becomes the model for the modern screen

psycho. The low-key, unassuming mild-mannered man who becomes a killing fiend for no apparent reason was envisioned long before Norman Bates. Also, the recent DVD release of *The Lodger*, starring Laird Cregar as Jack the Ripper, becomes a model for the modern horror movie psycho. Cregar's character "Slade" is very timid and withdrawn, a very private, antisocial man who lives in an attic apartment in a rooming house. His character "Slade" is damaged psychologically, having loved his brother (commentator Greg Mank implies the two shared a sexual attraction) who was destroyed by evil women, thus prompting Cregar's Ripper to avenge his brother's death by murdering "actresses" (since prostitutes would not have been cleared by the Production Code). So Laird Cregar's shy performance is psychologically based, and he uses a blade to carry out his carnage. Isn't this the model for Norman Bates? Greg Mank declares *The Lodger* to be the best horror film of the 1940s (I do not agree, but many agree with Mank), and being a major release by 20th Century Fox, the film had mainstream appeal and notice.

Mark: In fact, I'm hard pressed to think of another film that has had so profound and enduring an effect in shaping the horror genre, except maybe *The Cabinet of Dr. Caligari* (1919), which also didn't appear on your list—but I understand you were limiting the field to talkies.

Gary: Intelligent observations about *Psycho*'s influence on the modern horror film, but I still stand by my published 13 and maintain strongly that *Psycho* should not bump any of my choices. Here's why.

I defined *influential* thus: "My thesis would concern those groundbreaking horror movies that pushed the genre ahead creatively into new vistas of artistic expression. Movies that ignited sub-genres or created a new type of horror movie and were not one of a kind but became movers and shakers that inspired a slew of many others."

As I said, *Psycho* was on my short list, but I finally decided that the 13 titles I had all needed to stay. *Psycho* is indeed a horror classic, but it is mainly a *stand-alone* classic and an influential horror movie only in the secondary sense.

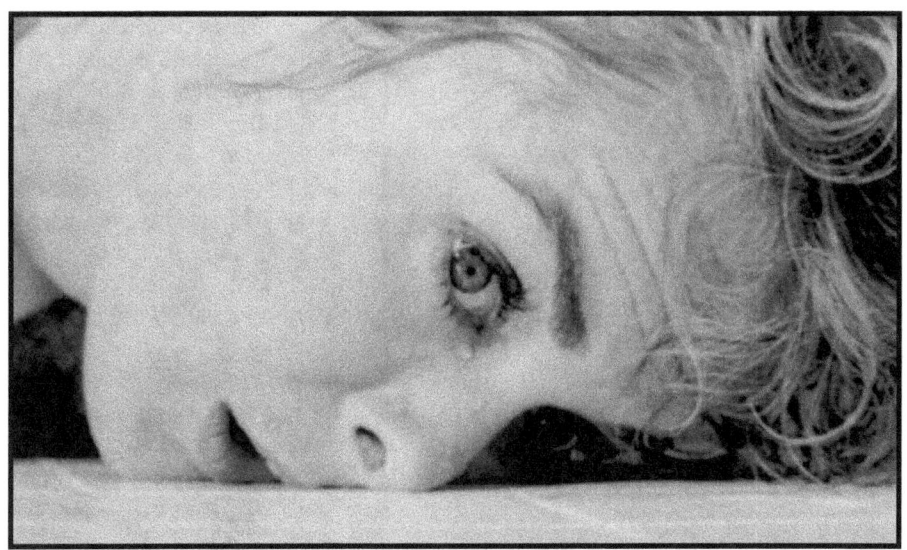

A closeup of the dead, open-eyed and naked Marion Crane.

In the article, I defined influential horror movies as movies that led to a new way of making horror movies—a new movement, a new vision. Here's an example. The Val Lewton RKO horror factory countered the juvenile Universal monster rallies of the 1940s with scripts with a more adult appeal. Monsters were gone; internal, psychological horror replaced the latex beasties (thus the seeds of *Psycho* are sown!). Something new was created as a reaction to the more traditional Universal vision of old. The Lewton style became easily identifiable and applica-ble to films not made by the Lewton unit. Diverse films such as *Night of the Demon* (*Curse of the De-mon* [1958]), *Night Tide* (1961), and *The Haunting* (1963) were all labeled Lewtonesque. The Lewton style can still be found in movies made today.

As a critical and financial hit, *Psycho* naturally begat other movies. Fans might say that *Psycho* directly influenced William Castle's *Homicidal* and *Strait-Jacket* (1964). But to me this "influence" is something a little different—an example of exploitation moviemaking. Castle copied a far superior movie to make a quick buck and made *Psycho* "knockoffs" rather than films that were influenced artistically by the Hitchcock classic. In the same vein, when *The Exorcist* was an artistic and financial hit, Ovidio Assonitis made *Beyond the Door* (1974), and producers recut and shot extra footage for Mario Bava's 1972 film *Lisa and the Devil*, rechristening it *House of Exorcism*, in order to ride the Satanic-possession wave. Neither Assonatis nor Bava's producers were *influenced*—as I define the term—they were cashing in on or exploiting the original *Exorcist*. The blaxploitation film *Abby* (1974) did the same thing. Can you see that subtle difference?

Probably 15 cheap-jack science-fiction movies (at least) came out in the wake of *Alien*. Was that "influence"? Cashing in on a hit movie is not quite the same as a hit movie influencing a new movement of creative merit. Exploitive knockoffs speak of lowbrow influence; my article speaks of highbrow influence. There's a difference.

Steven: I think there is the slimmest of lines, Gary, between influencing and exploiting. If you are inclined to discount the William Castle knockoffs, then I think the

Norman watches quietly from a window in his home behind the motel.

same argument can be made about the many slasher films released in the wake of *Halloween*, which is on your list. How many of them can truly be judged to be influenced "artistically" by these earlier films?

Gary: To quote from my definition again, "Influential movies are not necessarily great or archetypal, but they do create a sub-genre or a new way of doing horror that many others follow." *Halloween* and the movies it influenced meet the criteria of my definition. Let's talk about the American slasher movie. *Halloween* is the movie I most credit with influencing the slasher genre. No, it wasn't the first, but its financial success and artistic vision shaped the genre for a generation or more. *Psycho* was too classy, and its chief image was that of a drag-queen fiend parading around the house dressed as mother. It wasn't the dark-cloaked stalker of the modern slasher variety. In fact, the image of Norman Bates most of us have is of a momma's boy, shy and stuttering, who speaks quietly about stuffing birds. The image of Michael Meyers is not the same as Norman Bates. Hitchcock was most concerned with inner demons, which he exposed by probing Bates' persona psychologically—if rather clunkily, as the ending of his movie proves. But Meyers influenced psychos in cinematic slasher history with his silent stalkings, supernatural ability to appear and disappear, super-human strength and the soulless and ruthless killing-machine persona. Jason Voorhees was cast in the same mold. Norman Bates was a three-dimensional character…the modern slasher is more primal.

The question is not whether *Psycho* influenced other films but whether it belongs as one of the 13 most influential horror movies ever produced. "Influenced" can be defined in many ways, but I specifically defined what I was looking for. And exploitive knockoffs don't count in my definition of influence. And "top 13" means *Psycho* could be endlessly influential… but not as much as these 13.

Arthur: Okay, now I've got a handle on what you were trying to get across. "What did *Psycho* do to actually create a new movement in horror movies?"

Psycho was the first film to violate the contract that Hollywood had always made with us, that we in the audience would be protected. That, if we were asked to empathize with a protagonist—a main character—that character was going to be all right. We in the audience were going to be safe investing ourselves in that character right up until the end. In the end, there might be a macabre twist (à la *All Quiet on the Western Front* [1931] or *Sands of Iwo Jima* [1949]), but up until the last reel a main character was going to be spared anything really awful. But, when the protagonist of *Psycho* dies halfway into the movie, audiences

Birds are not the only formerly living creatures that have been "stuffed" by Norman.

were suddenly exposed and vulnerable. Anything could happen. Anyone could die at any moment, for no good reason.

I think Hitchcock took this a step farther in *The Birds* (1962), treating Tippi Heddren as a Hollywood goddess, then having her pretty face brutally injured by the birds. Again, our protective contract with Hollywood was violated, and we were left exposed to the fear of, moment to moment, what might happen.

This is the force that drives *Night of the Living Dead* (1968), in which we will see a lot of blood, where sympathetic characters are going to be killed and devoured, where our initial protagonist quickly becomes traumatized and where the one person we trust to survive the night is finally lost for no good reason.

That is what I was talking about when I originally brought up De Palma. He is a director who seemed to take an actual pleasure in making us empathize with a character, and then subject them to humiliation, violence and pointless death.

Finding new ways to violate the Hollywood contract was the driving force behind cinematic horror into the 1970s and beyond. Whether it was *Alien* (1979) killing off anyone who might survive or the wholesale bloodletting of *Tomb of the Blind Dead* (1971) and its sequels or every post-*Carrie* horror movie springing another shock after we should be safe (which has caused a new movie contract: there *will* be a shock just before the end), they are all following the path laid out by *Psycho*.

Mark: Gary, I recall your definition of "influential," and I would argue that *Psycho* did "push the genre ahead creatively into new vistas of artistic expression" and "ignited sub-genres," as I already spelled out. However, it's important to remember that artistic influence is not always direct, A to B. It may be A to C through B. For example, to draw a musical analogy, you may not listen to Oasis and think of Bob Dylan. Mid-period (*Revolver*-era) Beatles admittedly influenced Oasis, and Bob Dylan profoundly influenced the Beatles during this era. John and Paul's admiration for Dylan's work inspired them to create more meaningful and more personal lyrics, and expand their musical palate. Also, Dylan personally introduced the Beatles to marijuana and psychedelics, an experience that led in a direct line to *Revolver*.

Gary: So Mark, you point is that Bob Dylan influenced Oasis, sorta once removed, serving as an analogy to *Psycho* influencing other films in this same once

removed manner. I think, in the best interest of logical and rational thinking, that all we can say here is that the mid-period Beatles influenced Oasis. And that Bob Dylan influenced mid-period Beatles. But to make the jump and claim that Bob Dylan influenced Oasis is a logical fallacy that does not hold up well under close scrutiny. But please continue with your thesis here.

Mark: I think you see this sort of thing frequently with *Psycho*, with the slasher genre, for instance. For me, the line is from *Psycho* through Bava to *Friday the 13th*. There's no apparent direct connection between *Friday* and *Psycho*. But *Friday* was influenced by Bava's *giallo* thrillers (particularly *Bay of Blood* [*Twitch of the Death Nerve* (1971)]), and Bava freely admitted the debt he owed to Hitchcock in general and *Psycho* in particular;

Psycho's influence on the *giallo* film is pervasive. And I believe that clearly it was *Psycho* in particular and not Hitchcock films in general that provided the spark. For starters, you didn't see a wave of psycho killer movies kicked off by, say, *Strangers on a Train* (1951). The wave began with *Psycho*. Moreover, there are elements that appear only in *Psycho* that became *giallo* trademarks—the vicious but intricately crafted murder/set-pieces. Or the way the camera lingers, almost lovingly, over the dead body of Marion Crane at the conclusion of the shower scene. This long last look became a trademark of the *giallo*.

Gary: Not so fast, Mark! *Strangers on a Train* exists in the world of film noir and the noir psychopath existed since early 1940s cinema (*Stranger on the Third Floor* and *I Wake Up Screaming* initiated the trend). During the middle and late 1940s we had psychopathic fiends in noirs and mysteries such as *The Spiral Staircase; Somewhere in the Night; Sorry, Wrong Number; The Blue Dahlia; The House on Telegraph Hill; Where Danger Lives*. And while Hitchcock's psychopaths of *Strangers on a Train* were themselves influenced by these movies, *Strangers on a Train* influenced cinematic psychos as seen in early-mid 1950s movies as *The Big Combo, Ring of Fear, On Dangerous Ground, Night of the Hunter, While the City Sleeps*. So *Strangers on a Train* may be more influential than you are willing to admit (though, I will admit that the film noir/mystery psycho trend was not influenced *solely* by *Strangers on a Train*, of

Marion (Janet Leigh) and Sam (John Gavin) conduct their tawdry hotel affair in this well-lit publictiy shot.

course). But my point is that, outside of the horror film genre, many psychologically damaged fiends with knives were prevalent in the wake of *Strangers on a Train*.

Mark: I stand by my statement that *Baby Jane* was one of many black-and-white psychological thrillers that were issued in the wake of *Psycho*. No, it wasn't a cheap knockoff like *Homicidal*, but it tried to do exactly what *Psycho* did so successfully: Take a traditional Gothic sensibility, transplant it to an everyday modern setting and replace the old-fashioned monster with a deranged killer. *Baby Jane* in turn spawned a whole sub-genre. But, when you look at something like *Hush, Hush, Sweet Charlotte*, again I think you're seeing A influencing C through B. Even you grant the obvious visual similarities in the opening murder scene of *Hush, Hush*.

But the fact is that *Psycho*'s influence wasn't limited only to the *giallo*/slasher/psycho-killer genre. Many horror films have copied elements from or even the basic structure of *Psycho*. For instance, *The Ghoul* (1975). At first glance, especially given the presence of Peter Cushing, this film appears to be something inspired more by Hammer than Hitchcock. But take a look at the basic construction of the film: Our POV character at the opening of the film is a young blonde woman traveling across country in her car. She's forced to stop for the night, and is murdered. (By an unidentified killer, with a knife, through a shower-curtain-like veil surrounding her bed, no less.) A man and a woman follow to investigate what happened to her. The only thing missing is the revelation that Cushing himself is the killer—which would probably have been a more satisfying denouement than the one *The Ghoul* offers. This is just one particularly blatant example. There are countless more subtle ones (even without invoking De Palma's filmography).

Gary: No, no, I still stand by my published 13 and maintain strongly that *Psycho* should not bump any of my choices. Mark, which one of the 13 would you bump and replace with *Psycho*?

Mark: Look, I'm not necessarily arguing that *Frankenstein Meets the Wolf Man* and some of these other films weren't *un*influential. I'm arguing that *Psycho* had much greater influence.

Gary: Mark, you still insist that *Psycho* is one of the top four influential horror films of all time. The problem is that many films of this ilk were released during the same period of time, and that *Psycho* alone did not influence as many films as you would imagine. For example, Michael Powell's *Peeping Tom* (1960) was actually released within one month of *Psycho*. Of course, it did not generate the same box-office action, but Powell's film is very influential as far as psychos in film go, perhaps just as influential as *Psycho*.

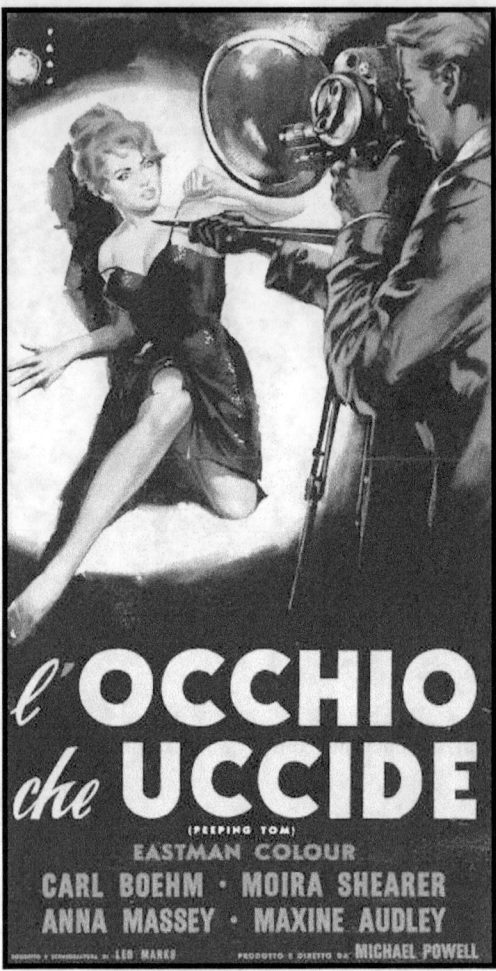

A foreign poster for Michael Powell's *Peeping Tom*

Mark: *Peeping Tom* was quite influential in its own right—although more for the way it helped form future filmmakers like Martin Scorsese than for any actual influence on the horror genre specifically. *Psycho* was a pop-culture phenomenon from day one and changed the character of horror cinema overnight. *Peeping Tom* made very little immediate cultural impact and was hardly ever seen for decades, although it enjoyed a belated critical resurgence thanks to film schools and the patronage of the cognoscenti, like Scorsese.

Gary: Sometimes art house pictures can be just as in-fluential as mainstream blockbusters, but in more subtle ways. Saying *Peeping Tom* made very little immediate cultural impact is opinion and seems a quick brush-off to Michael Powell's classic. Tell me, how many transsexual psychos appeared in cinema in the wake of *Psycho* (excluding knockoff copycat films such as *Homicidal*)? How many films about mother-fixated young men arrived in *Psycho*'s wake? How many films offering detailed, clinical, psychological explanations for the killer's actions arrived in *Psycho*'s wake? How many films, in *Psycho*'s wake, boasted that their leading lady was killed off halfway through the movie?

How many movies, created in *Psycho*'s wake, featured taxidermy?

Mark: How many films featured taxidermy? Oh, come on, Gary! Do we say that Howard Hawks' *The Thing* wasn't influential because few other films featured killer vegetables from outer space? Sure, many films copied elements, plot points and even some of the structural mechanics of *Psycho*. But the picture's influence goes far beyond that. *Psycho* brought Gothic horror into the modern era. It's the movie where the serial killer began to replace the vampire as our supreme bogeyman. Norman Bates is the new Dracula.

Brian: I wouldn't measure the impact of *Psycho* by how many movies copied its plot points (although Brian De Palma has used virtually

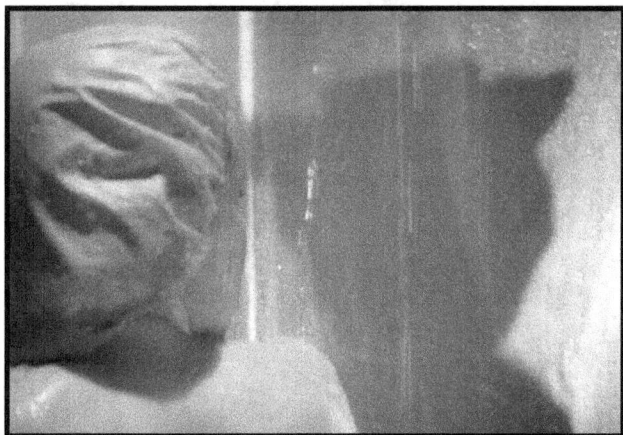

The Seventh Victim: The image of the silhouetted shadow menacing the vulnerable female in the shower and the young girl's fearful expression reminds us that shower horror began here.

every one—except maybe the one about taxidermy). I think it has more to do with expanding the horror film in new directions. Upping the ante on the degree of explicit violence acceptable. Forever removing the halo of protection that once surrounded major stars in sympathetic roles. And establishing at least one durable horror-movie cliché—the threatened woman in the shower. (I've seen *The Seventh Victim* several times but don't even remember that it *has* a shower scene.)

Arthur: The hell with showers, Psycho shows *toilets*! Flushing toilets! People reaching into flushed toilets! Breaking the unspoken agreement that Hollywood would never offend our eyes with such nasty things and making millions of shocked moviegoers cry out in unison "Eeeeewwwwwwwwwwww!"

Gary: See, I view *Psycho* as a stand-alone film because it is so original in both style and execution… Hitchcock was a master! Psychos with knives appeared in cinema both before and after the Hitchcock movie. Remember it or not, but the shower sequence in the critically underappreciated *The Seventh Victim* is a suspense nail-bitter. Even Hitchcock's *Rope* (1948) and *Strangers on a Train* dealt with deeply psychologi-

Norman chats up Marion Crane at the Bates Motel.

cally troubled killers (as did *Vertigo* and *Rear Window*). *Psycho* was a smash hit by a renowned director, and—when he had his killer use a knife—it resonated more. But influencing an artistic trend? I think you are confusing box-office hit with influential trendsetter. And I would argue that *Peeping Tom* is just as influential... for the very same reasons.

Brian: The killers in *Rope*, *Strangers on a Train*, *Vertigo*, and *Rear Window* aren't psycho killers. They may have psychological problems, but they all have strong motives for the murders they commit. They aren't lunatics compulsively murdering people. They're getting rid of inconvenient people, killing their wives or their mothers, and so on. The killers in *Rope* have a bizarre motive—proving their intellectual superiority—but they're not compulsive killers. I think you have to go back to *The Lodger* (1926) to find a true psycho-killer in Hitchcock's films prior to *Psycho*. And the main character in that film is an innocent man, who is suspected of being the killer.

Gary: And likewise, Brian, Norman Bates has a reason to kill. Remember, Bates has *become* mother and mother kills all the women who sexually arouse her innocent little boy Norman. She wants to keep Norman all to herself. She continues killing to protect her son. Mother's motives for murder are logical. I would argue that the killers you mention, Brian, are psycho killers, not any less so than Bates.

Arthur: And it's not *just* killing its main character halfway through the film that made *Psycho* such a groundbreaker; it's the feeling of unease that act created in the audience. After all, I believe that *Horror Hotel* (aka *City of the Dead* [1960], released three months after *Psycho*) killed its main character. However, no one that I know of came out of *Horror Hotel* feeling as defenseless as *Psycho* made them feel (I left *Horror Hotel* feeling positively exhilarated).

Arbogast (Martin Balsam) confronts Mother in a shocking overhead sequence, and he is sliced and dies a horrible death.

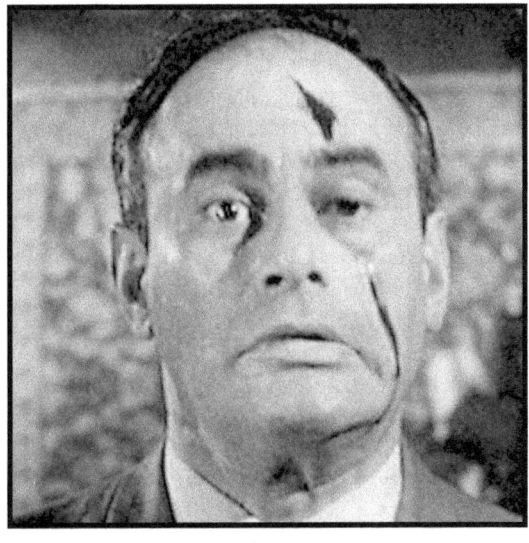

Gary: Arthur, this is quite subjective! *Horror Hotel* was *very* disturbing when it slaughtered its hot young college student midway through. And I felt more sympathy for her than I felt for Marion Crane. And Arthur, your reaction might be colored more by Hitchcock's stronger craft that better created that aura of defenselessness.

Arthur: I have to say it again, *Psycho* violated the agreement Hollywood movies had with us in the audience that nothing bad was going to happen to the person we'd been asked to empathize with. First, the film asks us to empathize with Janet Leigh and her plight of running away with money that wasn't hers. When she is killed, it not only kills the character we identify with, but the entire embezzlement plotline vanishes, never to be heard from again. We are off balance, not sure just what kind of movie we are watching.

Brian: Not only does the movie kill off the (presumably) lead character in the first half hour or so—her death is senseless. At this point, she's decided to go back to Phoenix and return the money. She's redeemed herself. And then she's murdered simply because she happened to stay in the wrong motel that night. She hasn't died for some greater, noble cause. Her death is meaningless and unfair. That's a transformative event in American cinema.

Arthur: The next person we start to empathize with is Detective Arbogast (Martin Balsam). This time we know a little more than Balsam does, and we are a step ahead

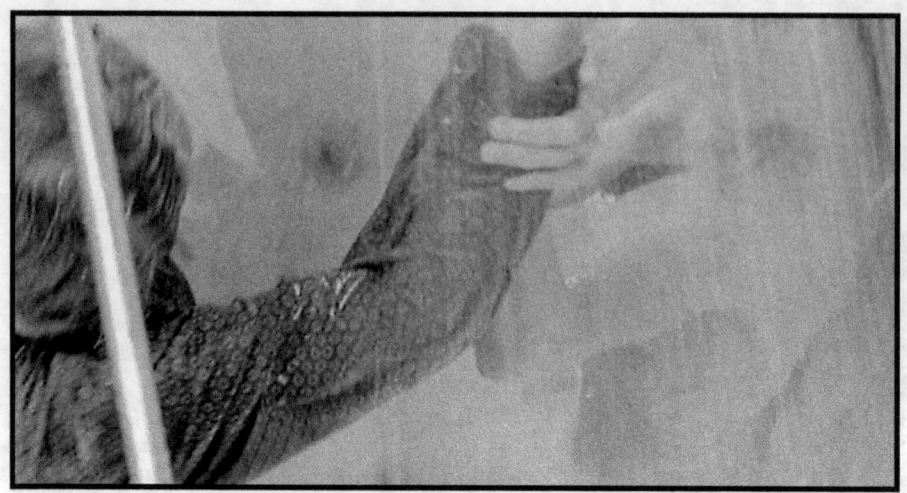
Marion struggles with "Mother" in the shower

of the game, so we watch helplessly as he dies because he doesn't know as much as we do.

We are next left with the chance to empathize with Lila Crane, Marion's sister (Vera Miles), and Sam Loomis, Marion's lover (John Gavin). Ah, but we've been burned that way before. If prior experience is any guide, they are going to end up dead with Leigh and Balsam. Instead, we take the safe choice, we empathize with Norman (Anthony Perkins). We already feel a little sorry for him; he has survived the movie so far; he'll probably get us through the movie in one piece. And that is the last card *Psycho* plays, the one person it has tricked us into empathizing with is the killer himself.

So it is not just the killing of the main character that makes *Psycho* a landmark, any more than it is the knife, or its transvestism or the fact that the bad guy is a psychopath. It is that the movie has violated our expectation of being taken care of. And it is that idea that begat *Night of the Living Dead* and *Carrie* and *Alien* and *The Hills Have Eyes* (1977), etc., etc., etc.

Bryan: Brilliant, Arthur! Bravo! I'm sold.

Gary: Bryan is correct, Arthur; your analysis is spectacular and worthy of an article in *Midnight Marquee*. I never quite heard that thesis stated in exactly that way before. Kudos. *Not* that I agree with your stated thesis, though.

Arthur: Thank you, Bryan and Gary, for all the kind words.

Anthony: Hey! Whadaya think *this* is?

Gary: —But to play Devil's Advocate for a minute, didn't films such as *The Leopard Man* (1943) and *I Wake up Screaming* (1941) play the same creative card by having the audience invest its sympathy in leading characters, both women, who are killed off halfway through? Was *Psycho* actually the first movie to trick its audiences in this way? Or was *Psycho* again influenced by earlier movies? Perhaps earlier movies that some of us may never have seen. The seeds of modern horror were planted during the 1940s!

Having seen *I Wake up Screaming* recently, I would have to say that, yes, it does produce an emotional impact comparable in 1941 (a tamer cinema era) to what *Psycho* did in 1960.

Anthony: Gary is right when he says we can find the roots of *Psycho* in earlier horror films like *I Wake up Screaming*. However, one could probably make that argument for almost *any* horror film.

Arthur: I would be the *last* person in the world to argue that *Psycho* wasn't influenced by earlier films. There's a shower scene in *The Seventh Victim* and in *Screaming Mimi* (1958). There are moments in *Bluebeard's Ten Honeymoons* (1960) that seem to come inches from being moments in *Psycho*.

The modern psycho perhaps begins with James Bell's low-key performance as the fiend in *The Seventh Victim*.

My point is simply this: which one of those films worked so hard to strip away the protections we relied on Hollywood to keep us safe with? Which one of those films had the unforgettable emotional impact of *Psycho*? What movie put all the pieces together and changed the way movies were made?

Gary: Humm, I would still select *The Seventh Victim*, *The Leonard Man* or *I Wake up Screaming* as the originators of this and not *Psycho*, and think Arthur's gushing over *Psycho* is merely how the film affected him emotionally. Perhaps people are giving *Psycho* too much credit for repeating what earlier films did just as effectively. Lesser known films but still important, influential ones.

Anthony: To try an analogy, *Horror of Dracula* (on Gary's list) had its roots in Universal's *Dracula* and other vampire movies. But it's what Hammer did with *Horror*—how it took the Dracula legend and vampires in general in a new direction—that makes the movie influential, right?

Steven: No movie exists in a vacuum, Gary. Was *Frankenstein* (also on your list) the first film to depict a corpse-like being returning to life? Was *Horror of Dracula* the first to explore the dark allure of the vampire? Respectfully, you can always play connect-the-dots and find another movie with plot similarities, especially now that we have decades of cinema history behind us.

Gary: You're missing the point guys. I too have moved beyond plot points and now am speaking of the emotional wallop and aura of unease felt by the vulnerable movie spectator long before *Psycho* arrived. No movie exists in a vacuum—but, Steven, Arthur's point was that this was a cinematic first and was the first time a name star, a "hero-

ine" (which I would disagree with), was killed off halfway through the movie. In *I Wake up Screaming*, alluring Carole Landis was the halfway-through victim! The young college student killed halfway through in *Horror Hotel* is much more sympathetic than Marion Crane in *Psycho,* and her death is very shocking and emotionally draining because of her vulnerability and unexpected demise. Arthur made a point, and I addressed his point.

Steven: Perhaps I misunderstood the thrust of Arthur's argument. But to me, the real influence of *Psycho* goes beyond mere plot points. It has more to do with the unsettling mood that hangs over the film, the feeling that the real horror never goes away. This would soon become the overall defining rule for the modern horror film. And I believe *Psycho*, as much as any other movie, is where it all begins.

Arthur: Again, let me say, did either *I Wake up Screaming* (which I've never seen) or *Horror Hotel* have the emotional impact of *Psycho*? Did either of them leave their audiences in such a quivering, swollen state? I think not.

Gary: Arthur, how do you know that?!!!! *Psycho* was a classic and did bring the Gothic age to modern times, to a point. But so did *Eyes Without a Face*, *Peeping Tom* (I say its influence is much stronger than Mark thinks), *The Sadist* (1963)...

Arthur: Oh yeah! *The Sadist*! I'd forgotten about that film. But isn't *The Sadist* a 'way-above-average *Psycho* knockoff? Right down to the title? Come on, the way it kills a main character very early on, and has two police officers who are shot down for no good reason—damn, it even kills off its male lead—isn't it simply carrying on the artistic movement that *Psycho* started?

Gary: What "artistic movement"? *The Sadist* managed to bring the Gothic fiend into the modern rock'n'roll world! Okay, *The Sadist* is an exploitive knockoff, copy-cat film made in the wake of *Psycho*, much like the higher-brow *Homicidal*. I have to admit that. But, again, copycat exploitive films are influenced monetarily and not artistically. They are influenced by the outer shell and not the inner artistic resonance.

Arthur, I saw *Psycho* in the theater…at its first re-release a few years after its initial release. And I did not know a thing about the film, including the surprises. But, compared to other horror films I saw in theaters, *Psycho* was less shocking than many others that I saw at a young age.

While I was terrified by earlier horror films, *Psycho* never really created in me that feeling that I could never feel safe watching a movie ever again. Hitchcock is a master

Norman/Mother struggles with Sam Loomis (John Gavin) in the cellar, at the climax.

at dread and suspense, and *Psycho* demonstrates his mastery. But we are really pushing things when we say that *Psycho* is influential because of its air of dread and because it created an unsafe feeling. Hitchcock's masterpiece does this well, but horror films have been doing that for ages. I myself found *Psycho* to be slightly meandering and perhaps too character driven and plot heavy. (For example, the doctor's explanation of Bates' problem at the very end was a major flaw and only proves that *Psycho* sometimes becomes too talky.) The major suspense scenes and cinematography are outstanding, but, if you see the film again, see if you don't look forward to the next "gripping" sequence while in between plodding through the sometimes overstated dialogue. My point is that your feeling of malaise, of ultimate dread, is based upon—admit it or not—the leading lady being killed halfway through the production, followed by Martin Balsam's equally sudden demise. But this wasn't the first, or last, time in cinema that two major characters were killed shockingly, surprisingly. *Psycho*'s air of never feeling safe is one of degrees; to say that *Psycho* initiated this feeling in other films is a flimsy way to try to uphold its influential status. *The Haunting* (1963)—not influenced by *Psycho* in the least—does precisely what you claim *Psycho* does, only better, but I would not say that *The Haunting* was influential because it was the first film to make audiences feel unsafe. But it accomplished exactly that.

Too many people here are confusing influential movies with blockbuster movies that inspire exploitive knockoffs. Blockbusters are not necessarily influential, but blockbusters always generate exploitive copycat variations.

Steven: But doesn't that argument shoot down your rationale for the inclusion of *Frankenstein Meets the Wolf Man* as one of the most influential horror films of all time? As much as I enjoy the escapism of *Frankenstein Meets the Wolf Man*, I see no artistic aspirations in this, and the subsequent monster rallies, whatsoever. To me, these films are Exhibit A when it comes to "exploitive copycat variations."

We can define "influential" in a variety of ways. The meaning that resonates most with me is that a film must tap into the pulse of the culture and, by doing so, forever

A foreign lobby showing a superimposed image of Norman juxtaposed against a ruthless Marion holding her ill gotten gains.

alter the expectations of the audience in its wake. This impact may be obvious (e.g., a series of copycat films) or it may be below the surface. Although *Psycho* did not spawn a spate of cross-dressing killer movies, I would argue that it certainly fulfills the latter condition. After *Psycho*, horror films were not "safe" anymore. A moviegoer now had to be on guard for the cinematic sucker punch—that moment in which we realize that the things we were led to believe were false or, at best, half-truths. Sure, there were films that explored this territory before but *Psycho* brought it to the forefront and made it a "new" cliché of horror cinema.

Gary: First of all, *Frankenstein Meets the Wolf Man* was produced by the same company that produced the original classic horror films, and the examples we are citing here are when lower-rent production companies exploit the work of more mainstream productions. Such is not the case here. How can Universal exploit itself? Instead, Universal re-visioned its early monster icons for a new generation of mostly younger fans. And the blending of multiple monsters became an artistic trend to this day (the latest being *Aliens vs. Predator: Requiem* that opened on Christmas Day 2007), thus justifying my inclusion of *Frankenstein Meets the Wolf Man* in my top-13 listing.

Second, let's play fair here.

Mark initiated this entire discussion in reaction to my *Midnight Marquee* article and my definition of the most influential movies. Anyone may define the term as he/she wishes, but, insofar as this ongoing discussion is concerned, let's stick to the one definition, so as not to confuse things. If this forum allows individuals to both redefine "influential" and argue for or against examples that fit their own definition, then in affect we are debating two things at once and arguing apples and oranges, invalidating the purpose of this discussion… a reaction to my article.

Mark: I beg to disagree with that request. The reasons why many of us disagree with your choices, Gary, is that many of us disagree with your definition of "influence," which is a much wider and more subtle term than the one that you used in your article.

As I see it, the whole ball of wax should be fair game.

Gary: By *any* definition I don't believe that *Psycho* belongs in the top 13, let alone the top four.

Mark: You are, of course, welcome to stand by that position. I feel compelled, however, to point out that you're standing there alone at this point!

Gary: So was Henry Fonda in *The Ox-Bow Incident,* where the majority view was *wrong*!

Let's pull from these threads all the so-called influences that *Psycho* created, and examine the skein. If I leave out any argument, please add on.

1. *Giallo* films from Italy. Okay, I accept that *Psycho* was one (of many) influences, but most writers credit (and rightfully so) Hitchcock's entire work as inspiration for *giallo* movies. The lush, dream-like cinematography and the doubling and obsession themes come from *Vertigo*. We have the claustrophobia of *Rear Window* with the slightly twisted good guy (also a carryover from *Vertigo*). The chase and suspense come from *North by Northwest* (1959). The stalking-in-the-shadows killers come from *The Man Who Knew Too Much*. And the influences go on and on.

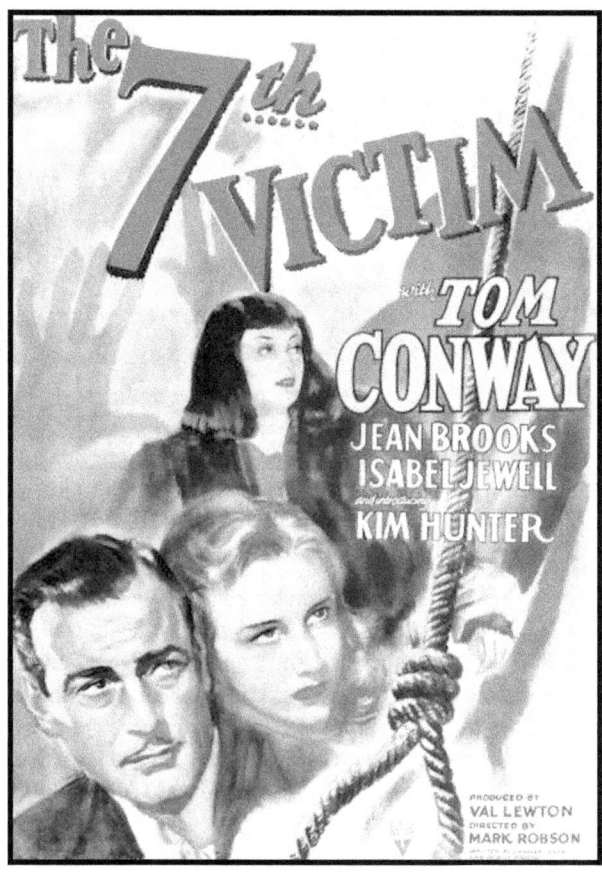

Psycho was just *one* film that influenced the *giallo* movement.

Mark: You're missing several things that people have mentioned. First of all, the whole slasher genre, which wouldn't exist without the *giallo*, which wouldn't exist without *Psycho*. (A to C through B, remember?)

Gary: I have difficulty accepting your A to C through B logic, remember??????!!!!!

Mark: Even you grant that *Psycho*, more than any other film, merged the Gothic with the contemporary and replaced the vampire/supernatural monster with the serial killer. But you don't seem to grasp the full implications of this. It would take another 20 years for all the ramifications to be felt, but films influenced by *Psycho* and films influenced by films influenced by *Psycho* completely reshaped the genre. *Psycho* was the first spear in the side of the traditional, period Gothic horror film. The innovations it launched eventually consumed the classic horror style. The death of classic horror, and birth of modern horror, is *Psycho*.

Also, I agree entirely with Arthur regarding *Psycho*'s postmodernist challenge to audience expectations.

Gary: I think the argument could be made that a *series* of films that include *Psycho* initiated the birth of the modern horror film (*The Leopard Man, The Seventh Victim,*

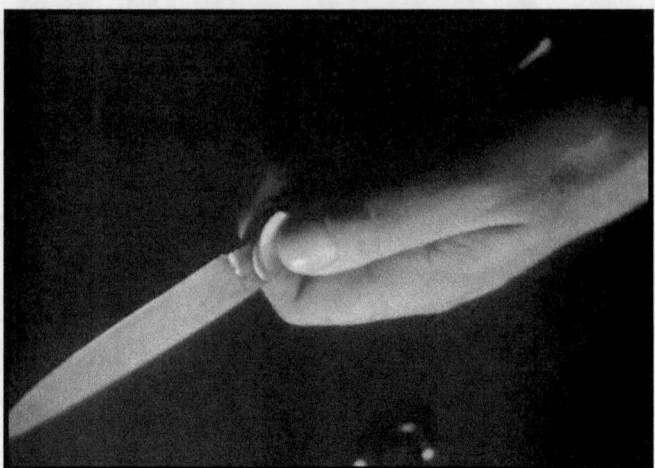

The Seventh Victim: The image of the killer and his knife permeated the screen long before *Psycho*.

Psycho, Eyes Without a Face, Peeping Tom, etc.).

I continue:

2. The copycat William Castle knockoffs including *Homicidal* and *Strait-Jacket*. Castle did not imitate *Psycho*'s inner resonance and artistic core but instead copied the external machinations and commercial frills...with the intent of making a buck. His exploitation films did him proud. So, in a sense, *Psycho* "influenced" such movies—agreed.

3. The Hammer psychological movies such as *Scream of Fear* and *Paranoiac*, which in turn were imitated and knocked off by Hammer's chief knockoff company, Amicus. So here's the question: Did the Hammer films influence the Amicus or were the Amicus psychos influenced directly from *Psycho*?

Mark: It doesn't matter if *Psycho* influenced the Amicus films directly or indirectly; the influence stems from *Psycho* originally. (A to C through B, remember?)

Gary: By this logic we could say Beethoven influenced Bob Dylan. By your A to C through B logic, every artist influenced every other artist through time and memoriam!

I will say that *Psycho* did influence the Hammer films.

4. The cinema of Brian De Palma. Again, his obsession with Hitch did not primarily focus on *Psycho*. He was just as influenced by all the other films mentioned in #1 above, although *Psycho* was one of his influences, granted. *One*!

Brian: Well, gosh, Gary, if you agree that *Psycho* influenced all of these types of films, what's your argument? That *Psycho* wasn't the sole influence? No one is saying that *Psycho* is the only influence on these films. But *Psycho* sure seems to be the common denominator here.

Gary: Brian, I never said that *Psycho* wasn't an influential film. I said that it does not belong in the top 13 influential horror films of the sound era.

No. Even though people are trying to hold on to Arthur's inspired theory (that *Psycho* was the first film to show audiences that they can never feel safe again), it seems far less credible the more I consider it. Other movies, such as *Horror Hotel* (released at the same time as *Psycho*), *I Wake up Screaming* and *The Leopard Man* tested the waters of killing off a sympathetic leading lady first. *The Seventh Victim* created the aura of audience's feeling unsafe, so much so that the sympathetic leading lady committed suicide at the film's finale in order to escape her life of torment (a life of torment that the audience felt as well). And I stress the word *sympathetic* here. Because, to further denigrate Arthur's logic here, I insist that *Psycho* never attempted to make us feel sympathetic for the murdered Janet Leigh character. That's the point of *Psycho*...no one is sympathetic. Janet Leigh plays a woman who is having an illicit sexual affair (as judged by the morality of the time) and steals money from her own company. She's a crook, for god's sake! Is this Hitch making us feel sympathetic toward her?

The "absolutely sympathetic" Marion Crane, looking great in her bra and half-slip.

Brian: Marion Crane is absolutely a sympathetic character, and not just because she looks great in bra and half-slip. She's in a difficult situation with her lover; she succumbs to temptation and steals the money. Audiences can sympathize with a character who does something wrong, if they understand the reason why she does it. Marion Crane is a good person who, in a moment of weakness, does the wrong thing. And she does redeem herself. During her conversation with Norman in the parlor, she decides to go back and return the money. Just before she goes back to her room, she tells Norman that she has a long drive ahead of her in the morning. Back home, to Phoenix. That's the significance of the scene when she's figuring out how much of the money she's spent so far—she's going to have to make up the difference when she gives the money back.

Hitchcock goes to great lengths to make Marion Crane a sympathetic character. And then, just when the audience should be completely sympathetic to her, she goes into that shower, and she's doomed.

When I saw *Psycho* for the first time, I knew Marion Crane was doomed from the beginning. It's hard for me to imagine the impact her death had on 1960 audiences, who were not expecting it.

Arthur: Well, the word I think I used was not "sympathize" but "empathize." We follow Janet Leigh's story. We see events through her eyes. An audience in the early 1960s is primed to empathize with the star of the movie. These are not the 1970s where the protagonist is often a bad guy. Illicit affair or not, we identify with Leigh.

Brian: I agree with your arguments, Arthur, but object to the term *illicit affair*. What, exactly, is the nature of this "illicit affair"? Sam is divorced. Marion is single. They live in different cities, so they meet in hotel rooms. Sam would marry her, but he can't because he's financially strapped—his income goes for alimony to his ex-wife.

Marion's sister Lila (Vera Miles) and Sam look to find Marion at the Bates Motel.

I wouldn't call that an illicit affair. Just a difficult situation—which Marion tries to resolve by stealing that money.

Arthur: I was quoting Gary, who called their unwedded romance an "illicit affair." My exact words were "Illicit affair or not"—i.e., I was not challenging whether the affair was illicit because my point stood either way.

In any case, a pre-sexual revolution audience was probably going to look upon any kind of sexual relationship outside of marriage as, at least, sordid.

Brian: I didn't pick up that you were quoting Gary when you used the term "illicit affair." And, yes, attitudes about pre-marital sex were different then than they are now. That's one of the reasons why the *Psycho* (1998) remake was so stupid—the sexual politics didn't make sense anymore.

But, even at that, Hitchcock goes a long way toward generating audience sympathy for Marion Crane, with that whole conversation she and Sam have about "respectability." Marion thinks this affair is a bit sordid, too. She doesn't want to be meeting Sam in hotel rooms for the rest of her life. Sam doesn't really want this, either; it's just that he's trapped in a bad financial situation. (I think, in addition to alimony payments, he's also paying off a bunch of debts he inherited from his father.)

Gary: To be honest, it's been a while since I saw *Psycho*, and I assumed that Sam Loomis was in fact married. I am mistaken on that point, granted. However, even if he is divorced, it just does not negate my terminology. Let me explain. The imagery of the voyeuristic camera creeping through the bedroom hotel window and catching the brazen woman in a bra and half-slip pre- or post-coitus creates an image of sleaze. How many married men claim to be divorced to seduce a woman? How many criminals claim they will return the money—tomorrow? Let's face it, the Catholic Legion of Decency with its dreaded *Condemned* label ruled Hollywood at the time. Outright adultery would have damned the movie if it were shown on screen.

Having the male profess to be divorced and the female vocally claim she would give the money back may have been more a concession to the censorship board than a softening of the two characters to make them sympathetic, as many claim.

Brian: Well, there's a world of difference between a single woman sleeping with a single man and a single woman sleeping with a married man—even in 1960. There is absolutely no hint in the movie that Sam is lying about being divorced. Agreed—the voyeuristic camera work at the beginning of the film creates an image of sleaze. But the dialogue between the characters undercuts the sleazy imagery. I think its clear that the audience is meant to like Marion Crane, if not necessarily approve of her actions or her morals.

Arthur: No argument here. My own point was that the film at the very least generates empathy with Marion Crane, which is close to sympathy, but I didn't want to confuse "sympathy" with "feeling sorry for," so I stuck with "empathy." There I go again, using quotation marks!

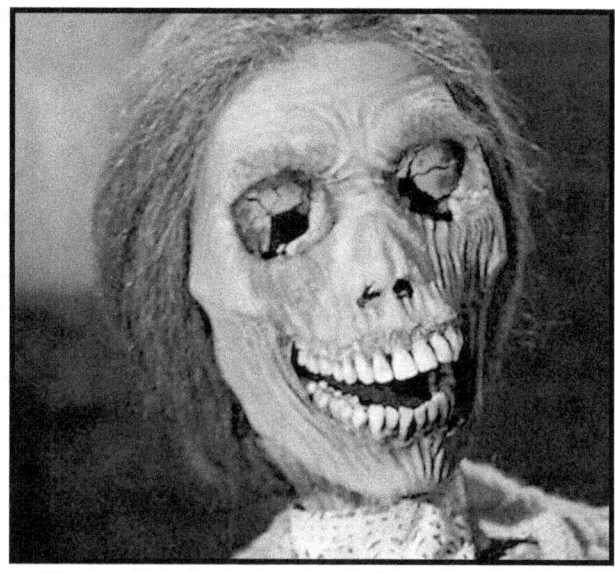

Norman Bates' actual mother, looking worse for wear.

Brian: I think we have to consider the Janet Leigh factor. She was a very popular and well-liked star at the time. I can't think of any movie she made prior to *Psycho* in which she didn't play a sympathetic character. Because Janet Leigh plays Marion Crane, audiences are primed to like her—and forgive her her transgressions—before the movie even begins.

Arthur: Illicit affair or not, we both agree about what *Psycho* does to a viewer. We do not watch the action of *Psycho* from a protective distance. At least not the first time. But, then, after we have been burned so badly for our identification with Leigh, the next time we watch the film it is from a protective distance. We have taken the first step to the films of the 1970s.

Gary: When she is slaughtered, are we sorry? I think we are surprised, perhaps even shocked, not sorry! Her murder is moral retribution for her sins, and, despite her stunning sexual pose in bra and half-slip, we must remember never to confuse lust with sympathy.

Arthur: "Sorry"? No, I think the audience feels totally shattered and betrayed.

And I don't think the film behaves as if her murder is any moral retribution. Remember, Leigh doesn't need to be taught a lesson. She has already decided to go home and face the consequences of her actions. That is why she takes the shower. It is symbolic of her washing away her sins. The film has given us every cue in the world that things are going to be all right. The last thing that should happen to her is her death.

No, I think there is nothing right or just about her murder. It is pure dumb luck in a random universe (a theme Hitchcock would return to in *Frenzy* [1972]).

But, we are not going to agree on this issue.

Gary: Arthur, I can only say again that I never had the sense of feeling shattered and betrayed by Crane's death as you had. It never rocked me in that way. I was always

The image of the knife plunging; the long arm housing female clothing to trick the audience.

more fascinated by her nudity, seeing if I could count the knife strokes. And watching the swirling tub water focus on the dead, open eye. With Hitch, it's always about the method, never the emotion.

I think you are making a personal reaction to a movie but trying to state it as a collective reaction ("I feel this way, so everyone must feel the same way").

Arthur: Oh, forget it; I'm just going to go slit my wrists.

Steven: But I feel the same way. I was going to say maybe I'm alone on this, but, after hearing Arthur and Brian, I see I'm not.

I certainly feel sympathy for Marion Crane. She's made mistakes (*big* ones!), but her choices are never made out of malice or lack of compassion for others. And there's that point in the film where her conscience gets the better of her and she decides to head back home and atone for what she has done...until the rug is pulled out from under her (and us).

Anthony: When I was teaching *Psycho* as part of a film course at Wayne State University back around 1980, I told my students how Hitchcock claimed that he wanted to kill Janet Leigh in such a startling, unexpected manner because, he said, once that happened, the audience would be off balance, not knowing what to expect from then on. (This remark seems to confirm Arthur's assessment of the movie's impact.) A woman in class (about my age at the time, maybe a little older) said, "I can confirm that." She explained that she had taken her 11-year-old son to class with her so he could see the film. Like everyone since 1961 at least, he knew about the infamous shower scene, and he was ready for it. After it took place, he told his mother, "Aw, mom, that wasn't so bad"—but, she said, from that moment on, until the end of the movie, he kept a tight grip on her arm.

I saw *Psycho* long after it was released, and on network TV, so it was interrupted by commercials and possibly censored (although I think I saw it on the Canadian station, which was/is more liberal than our local stations). I can't say I had the reaction that original viewers did or that my student's son did.

However, I can tell you a second-hand anecdote: a fellow I used to work with, Chuck Andersen, saw *Psycho* when it came out. He and three high school buddies drove downtown and saw it at the Palms in Detroit. They got out of the theater after dark and walked to their car in the parking lot. They just got in when a guy banged on their window and spooked the hell out of them. It was just a panhandler, but the movie experience had so unnerved them that they jumped and got out of there fast.

And, of course, reportedly, after *Psycho*, Janet Leigh always had the staff remove the shower doors when she stayed at a motel.

Gary: The stuff of which urban legends are made! I always felt this story was good PR copy and I never believed the hype.

Anthony: Arthur mentioned *Alien* in the same breath as *Psycho*, and I must heartily concur—at least in the effect that director Ridley Scott was striving for and achieved. The "chest-buster" sequence in *Alien* is akin to the shower scene in *Psycho*.

Once that happens, the viewer is thrown off balance and doesn't know *what* to expect for the rest of the movie. John Hurt seemed as if he might be the hero of the movie; he wasn't—he was killed off. Tom Skerrit, who definitely had to be the hero of the movie (he was the captain of the ship, right?) *also* wasn't: *he* was killed off. You never knew for sure if the last crewmember, Sigourney Weaver's Ripley, was going to survive or not.

Mark: Good comparison with *Alien*, which takes the *Psycho* structure to its logical endpoint.

Gary: I can confirm the same reaction to *Alien*. I went to the Uptown Theater, Washington D.C.'s premiere old movie palace, in 1979 with my teacher buddy Wayne Shipley (he's in both of our feature films). I was 29 years old, and the both of us were shocked out of our seats. For me I was *never* more frightened in a movie theater, and no movie ever frightened me as much as *Alien*. You never did know what was coming next and who would die. It was relentless tension and horror for two hours. *Psycho*, which I saw at age 13, never had that effect of terrifying me or making me feel constantly ill at ease. Not like the effect *Alien* had on me at age 29. I guess it just depends upon what frightens you the most. Again, that's why I find it so difficult to accept Arthur's theory...for *Psycho* never affected me like that.

The prologue to the shower murder sequence

Neil: I also had the same response to *Alien*—I think one great reason for that reaction was the fact we didn't see that chest burst in *every single ad and trailer* before the film was released, as we do now. Until the mid-1980s, you could still be surprised at a film (assuming you didn't read *Cinefantastique*). Thanks to ad campaigns and the net, we now have virtually no surprises left.

Steven: Spot-on, Neil. The overexposure of surprise sequences, punch lines and plot twists in trailers is one of many things that have soured me on the modern moviegoing experience.

Anthony: I appreciate Gary's story about *Alien*. I was nearly 31 when I saw it, and I remember the nervous laughter that followed after the chest buster burst through John Hurt and went skittering away. I would call the audience reaction "whistling in the dark." After the chest buster scene, despite people's bravado, the tension in the audience was even more palpable than before. Remember how nervous you were when Harry Dean Stanton was taking his (last) long walk alone? You knew he was gonna get it—but when? *When*? The scariest moment for me, I think, was the shock shot when Tom Skerritt, in the vents, lit his light, and suddenly the alien was behind him and upon him. Cut to black!

Gary: Look, Janet Leigh's death was shocking—I think I've already granted you that—but the degree to which it is shocking is open to debate and different opinions. The sequence does not register as high on my shockometer, nor does the feeling you state of never feeling safe again or never trusting our faith in our empathy with a leading character again. I bet you the next week or so after seeing *Psycho* you went right back out to the theaters and again put your faith completely in the protagonist and felt, wisely or not, that everything would turn out all right. Business as usual, right????

Even though Marion's change of heart before the murder attempts to soften the Crane character, I still find there to be no truly likable character in the movie (not that I dislike any or hate any…I just find everyone very flawed and lacking sympathy). And it was Sue [Svehla, *Midnight Marquee* co-editor] who alerted me to that point of view because she is sensitive to movies that lack sympathetic characters. She's into fuzzy bunny movies!

But I still maintain that the unsympathetic nature of Crane was created so the audience would not be overwhelmed with emotion when she is slaughtered. I think Hitchcock wanted to maintain that emotional distance (one of his signature mannerisms) so audiences could react to the shock of her death and not the sadness. Just as you mention about the Bates character, Hitch wanted all of us to be voyeurs.

Norman, always the voyeur, is ready for Sam's entrance at the Bates Motel office even before Sam is aware he is being eye-balled.

By the way, I always agreed that *Psycho* was influential to a degree, but that it exists mainly as a stand-alone horror-film classic, a one of a kind.

Anthony: True, *Psycho* is "a stand-alone horror-film classic, a one of a kind." But I bet that's something that we could say about many influential films. Many, if not most, truly influential films are indeed unique—what's the phrase? "often imitated but never exceeded," or something?—but that doesn't lessen their influence.

On the other hand, I should admit that I think I know what Gary is getting at—certain films are certainly unique, existing on their own plane, seemingly divorced from what's gone before and comes after them—but I wouldn't put *Psycho* in this particular category.

Gary: And I still stand by my claim. Arguments #1-#4 don't sway my opinion. Sorry.

Mark, I'll agree that *Psycho* is a pop-culture phenomenon, as you said earlier. But Norman Bates as the modern Count Dracula? Dracula was majestic, sexual, alluring, powerful and mesmerizing. Norman Bates was awkward, shy, low-key, tentative and powerless. Each is the antithesis of the other. Even if you consider Norman Bates a cultural icon of the modern horror movie in the way that Dracula was in the films of yesteryear, it does not mean the film is influential. Hannibal Lecter is an icon, but his movies are not influential, and one can make a better case that Hannibal is the Norman Bates of our generation than Bates was the Count Dracula of his.

Mark: What I meant when I said Norman Bates is the modern Count Dracula was not that Norman has any traits in common with Dracula. What I meant was that the vampire-to-serial-killer transition occurs, or at least is initiated, in *Psycho*. Norman Bates is the killer in *Psycho*. So he replaces Dracula in the post-Gothic paradigm, as the central villain in the most influential work.

Jonathan: If you ask me—and you didn't—there is simply no logic on the face of the Earth for excluding *Psycho* from a list of the most influential horror films.

Lila, in a close reaction shot, learns the truth of her sister's fate.

(Sorry, Gary.) Unless, of course, you make the argument, as James J.J. Janis has for years, that *Psycho* isn't really a horror film at all, but a crime film of some sort (a notion I reject personally, but it's a valid theory anyway).

Gary: Such absolute statements are always bound to get the speaker into trouble, don't you think? No, I say *Psycho* is a horror film. However, London's *Time Out* offers an interesting, alternative view of *Psycho*: as a black comedy!

"No introduction is needed, surely, for Hitchcock's best film, a stunningly realized (on a relatively low budget) slice of Grand Guignol in which the Bates Motel is the arena for much sly verbal sparring and several gruesome murders. But it's worth pointing out that Hitch was perfectly right to view it as fun; for all its scream of horror at the idea (and consequences) of madness, it's actually a very black comedy, titillating the audience with its barely linear narrative (the heroine disappears after two reels), with its constant shuffling of audience sympathies, and with its ironic dialogue ('Mother's not quite herself today'). Add the fact that we never learn who's buried in Mrs. Bates' coffin, and you've got a stunning, if sadistic, two-hour joke. The cod-Freudian explanation offered at the conclusion is just so much nonsense, but the real text concerning schizophrenia lies in the tellingly complex visuals. A masterpiece by any standard."

Mark: Oh, there's a *ton* of black comedy in *Psycho*. Although most of it isn't noticeable until you've seen the film a time or two and know that Norman and Mother are one in the same. In my book (*Smirk, Sneer, and Scream*—shameless plug!) I wrote about the subtleties in Anthony Perkins' performance that enable these comedic elements.

Gary: I was just trying to get a handle on the film's tone. Arthur argues that the film permeates the aura of ill-ease discomfort and feeling unsafe; yet now, arguments are made where the film's black humor is dominant. Humm…

Mark, because of your different way of looking at the definition of what constitutes an influential movie, you were able to see *Psycho* as an influence on the *giallo* film, which then inspired the slasher film of the 1980s. This logic works with your definition but less so with mine. You see, I tried to keep my influential definition simple, and let me quote from my article: "No, I was not speaking about my favorite films or even

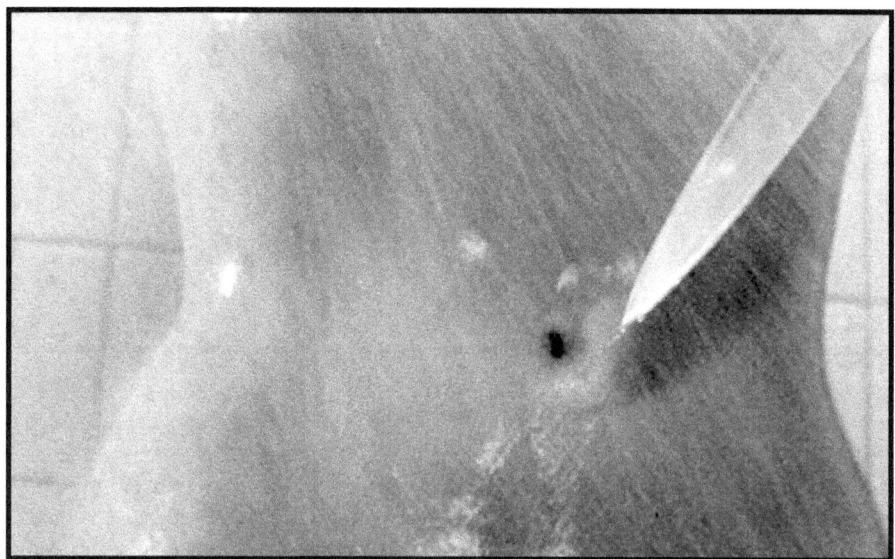
Hitchcock's imagery of naked flesh and the penetrating blade

the very best ones. My thesis would concern those groundbreaking horror movies that pushed the genre ahead creatively into new vistas of artistic expression. Those movies that ignited sub-genres or created a new type of horror movie that was not one of a kind but became a mover and shaker that inspired a slew of many others." And I set up the parameters of selecting only 13 movies released from 1930 until 2000. My definition of influential is more a direct influence, not the gestalt theory that a youthful Roger Corman went to the theater to see *Isle of the Dead* in 1945, which influenced him to make *House of Usher* a generation later. I wanted to keep my definition basic so that the 13 examples could be easily defined, explained and supported. This wasn't to be the six-degrees-of-Kevin-Bacon film analysis, because I believe that almost any film could be seen as influential with the more wide-open definition here put forth by you. Since I was limiting myself to 13 films, I needed a limiting definition.

Brian: I'm comfortable with your definition—and I believe *Psycho* qualifies as one of the most influential horror films using your definition.

Anthony: Is anyone familiar with the source novel? I ask because I thought it might shed some light on the character of Marion Crane (or whatever she's called in the book). How large a role does she play in the novel? Is she the focus of the first three-fifths of the story, as she is in the movie? Or is she more of a minor character? Is the focus on Norman Bates from the beginning? I ask, of course, because—if Marion's role was *enlarged* from what it was in the book, then Hitchcock and/or his screenwriter Joseph Stefano was making a conscious decision to expand the role for the purposes of playing a trick on—pulling the rug out from under—the audience. (If she *is* the focal point of the first part of the book, then Hitchcock's decision would have been to cast a popular starring actress in the role, even though he knew she wouldn't make it to the final reel. I mean, by rights, in the normal Hollywood course of things, Vera Miles' role and Janet Leigh's role should have been reversed: *Leigh* should have been the sister seeking her missing sibling.)

Mark: I bought a paperback copy of *Psycho* when I was in high school, which I started reading, lost interest in and then eventually lost track of. So I am *not* the best source of info! But I remember the novel being not very similar at all to the film. I don't remember Marion being in the story at all, but apparently she was because I've heard interviews with Stefano where he talks about expanding (rather than inventing) the character for the screenplay. Stefano always gave Hitch credit for the idea of knocking off the star a third of the way into the narrative.

Jonathan: Actually I have read the book, which is one of Bloch's lesser works, and it is pretty accurately transferred to screen—

Mark: Obviously, my memory is suspect.

Neil: I've always suspected that...

Jonathan: —hence Bloch's decades-long beef with Stefano, who tried to promote himself as the creator of *Psycho*. Mary Crane, as she is called in the book, is in it for roughly the same amount of time as Marion Crane is in the movie. Norman is more of a fat guy who keeps copies of Lovecraftian works of magical lore about the house, but, for the most part, I think Hitch follows the novel very closely. Except that, in the shower, Mary Crane is completely decapitated, heh heh…

Anthony: Thanks for the comments about *Psycho* the novel, Jonathan and Mark. ...So I guess Marion (Mary) was in the book and got killed, but did she have the same back story? Did the book start with her and then drop her?

Brian: The novel *Psycho* begins with Norman Bates—he's reading some book about Incan atrocities and really getting into it. Then it shifts focus to Mary Crane. In my copy of the book, she first appears on p. 15, and gets her head cut off in the shower on p. 37. So the movie expands on the Mary Crane character considerably. Otherwise, I think the movie follows the structure of the novel pretty closely.

Cindy: As I recall, the knife cuts off her scream...and her head. (I think that's the way Bloch puts it.)

Arthur: So the big innovation of the movie, starting one storyline and then abandoning it along with its protagonist, came from Hitchcock and Stephano.

Cindy: Yes. Actually, I wrote a piece on *Psycho* for Midmar's unfortunately unrealized Hitchcock book. Part of my discussion focused on what came from Bloch and what came from Hitchcock/Stefano.

One thing I can tell you, off the top of my mind, is that Stefano claimed that the innovation was *his* idea.

Norman reveals his inner "mother"

Jonathan: All of this rather long and convoluted discussion is probably beside the point; given the critical and cultural reaction to the Hitchcock film, debating its influence is kind of like asking how many angels can dance on the head of a pin.

Bryan: Well, I for one have immensely enjoyed the cogent back-and-forth arguments of Mssrs. Clark, Lundquist, and Svehla on this topic. Well done, gentlemen!

Anthony: Hey! What about the rest of us?

Mark: All this discussion is a testament to Gary's fine work on his original *MidMar* essay. The way I see it, any article that can generate this kind of passionate, informed debate must be a pretty damned interesting, provocative work. Nice job, Gary!

Gary: Mark, thanks for the kind remarks.

Brian: I've been enjoying this discussion immensely. It's great to argue about this stuff with knowledgeable people who love these movies as much as I do. This would be a pretty dull list if everybody agreed with everybody else about everything. And I appreciate Gary's willingness to take on all comers in our own little Battle Royale.

Gary: Let me say that I am impressed with many theories expressed here, even if I didn't buy all of them. Arthur, your passionate creation of how the tone of *Psycho* influenced the modern horror film had me thinking quite a bit. I did criticize the theory, I realize, but I wanted others to think as deeply as you did in perhaps addressing my critical affront.

Steven: And, Gary, thank you for taking the time to engage us in so lively a debate. As with all such discussions in fandom circles, I suppose that nothing much was settled.

Brian: Well, if things were ever settled by these sorts of debates, we'd have had to disband fandom years ago.

Long Live Unsettled Debates!

Gary: Nothing much was settled? That's for the reader to decide! You are all worthy adversaries. Feel free to bring it on next time, brothers and sisters!

HALLOWEEN SLICING AND DICING THE URBAN LEGEND

by Daniel J. Graffeo

I had the misfortune of witnessing *Halloween: Resurrection* on TV. Laurie Strode, played by Jamie Lee Curtis, the strongest character in the series, is killed off in 10 minutes. Michael Myers then encounters a mental patient that knows all about mass murderers. The mental patient takes one look at Myers and recites Myers's past like some horror version of Dustin Hoffman's *Rain Man*. Myers apparently is impressed by the psychotic fan's gruesome expertise—and gives him a butcher knife for a souvenir.

Michael Myers returns to his hometown in Haddonfield, Illinois, to kill more teenagers—but this time he does it live over the Internet. How very 21st century of him. Myers can't kill everyone though. We need at least two survivors. One is Sara Moyer, the down-to-earth, pretty heroine portrayed by Bianca Jahlich. The other is Freddie, the stereotypical black character played by Busta Rhymes. In one particular scene, Freddie dons the Michael Myers trademark coveralls and William Shatner mask in an attempt to scare up Internet ratings. When he encounters the real Michael Myers, Freddie believes it's one of his friends playing dress-up. Freddie proceeds to yell at Myers and shoves him for good measure. Myers walks away, confirming that we don't need a gun, an ax, the police or a scream queen to stop the Shape. We just need an angry cliché black man to scold him.

One can't help but wonder: When did the *Halloween* series fall apart? More importantly, can it get any worse? Will Busta Rhymes return to discipline Michael again? *Halloween: The Sensitivity of Michael Myers* might not be too far off!

This article discusses why the original *Halloween* is a classic horror film. It also shows why the sequels are not only inferior to the original, but how they have dragged a once potentially good series into inadequacy. *Halloween III: Season of the Witch* will be omitted because it's not an actual sequel to the Michael Myers saga and therefore has little value in this analysis. Director Rob Zombie's recent stand-alone remake of the original film will also be omitted, since his contribution is not part of the original franchise series.

As most critics agree, the first *Halloween* is still the best and makes many top-10 lists of the greatest horror movies. Although the script is simple, it is John Carpenter's exceptional direction that makes the film a classic. In the opening scene, we see someone entering the house, grabbing a butcher knife, going up to Judith Myers's bedroom, stabbing her to death, descending the staircase and exiting the front door, where the shocked victim's parents await. We discover that the killer isn't a typical kooky-eyed giggling man, but a blank-faced and silent six-year-old boy. Although the killer's identity suggests a different kind of psychopath from the mainstream Hollywood standard, it is the opening shot that lures the viewer. The opening sequence appears to be one continuous steadycam motion, which was a painstaking shot. Such an idea shows Carpenter's masterful talents that threaten to rival Alfred Hitchcock's. Unfortunately, such risky and creative camera shots died along with Judith Myers as no director in the series' sequels has ever attempted to try something that risky. It's a shame, because that particular opening scene shows us the murder through the killer's eyes. In a dramatic way, the viewer is the murderer whether he or she likes it or not. This can be unsettling to the sensitive spectator.

Another sensational camera shot is when Annie (Nancy Loomis) is in the kitchen pacing back and forth while talking to her boyfriend. Behind her is a pair of French doors. As she paces to the left, Myers appears behind the glass doors. As she paces right and goes to look out the doors, he is suddenly gone. As in the opening scene, this is one continuous shot that flows and, if watching for the first time, may give the viewer the impression that it was all a paranoid illusion. Yet, what gives Carpenter his edge in this film is not when we see the Shape's face, but when we *don't* see it. Most of the shots involve either seeing the back of the Shape's head or not seeing him at all, typically only hearing his breathing, such as the scene when Lynda (P.J. Soles) and Bob (John Michael Graham) are having sex.

In the sequels, the closest we come to Carpenter's gift for suspense with camera angles is seeing the victim in the foreground while the Shape's staring and blurry im-

Halloween: Director John Carpenter uses the darkness for each of the three major murders. We never see the knife go into the teen's torso.

age is in the background. In *Halloween 4: The Return of Michael Myers*, it was when Deputy Logan (George Sullivan) is sitting in the rocking chair by the front door. In *Halloween 5: The Revenge of Michael Myers,* it was Rachel Coruthers (Ellie Cornell) when she was dressing in her bedroom. In *Halloween: The Curse of Michael Myers*, it was Debra Strode (Kim Darby) talking on the phone with her angry husband (Bradford English). In *Halloween H20*, it was Nurse Marion (Nancy Stephens) investigating her burglarized house. The sequels had a higher budget than the original and needed to stick with techniques that producers knew worked, or else box-office money could be lost. The original *Halloween* was an independent film, which meant more freedom to take creative chances, and Carpenter's daring experiments made *Halloween* the most successful independent movie for years.

The movie's final moment is even more brilliant than the opening shot. Dr. Loomis, played by Donald Pleasence, looks over the balcony and sees that Michael Myers has walked away after being shot six times. John Carpenter mentioned that Donald Pleasence had two suggestions: "I can play this two ways. I can play this 'Oh my God!' or I can play this 'I knew this would happen.'" We also see a montage of possible places the Shape could be hiding while hearing his chilling breathing behind his mask. The breathing itself is noteworthy. It acknowledges the Shape's presence.

At the same time, *Halloween*'s effectiveness is its ability to make popular urban legends believable. The first urban legend is often entitled "The Babysitter and the Man Upstairs." The legend is about a babysitter who receives disturbing phone calls. She (the babysitter is always a young attractive girl, not unlike Laurie Strode) hears heavy breathing on the other end of the line. The babysitter calls the operator for assistance. The operator tells the babysitter that if the heavy breather calls again, to keep him on the line for as long as possible, while the call is being traced. Sure enough, another call occurs and the babysitter stalls the heavy breather until he hangs up. The operator

Halloween: Laurie Strode photograhed close up, while the formerly dead Shape rises up in the background.

immediately calls the babysitter and urges her to leave the house because the crank calls are coming from an upstairs extension. The babysitter survives the ordeal, like Laurie Strode, but bloodshed occurs: in the urban legend, the victims are children; in the movie, three teenagers appear. Two scenes occur where the breathing over the phone is implied. The first is after Laurie sees Michael Myers amid the flapping laundry on a neighbor's clothesline and the phone rings. The second is after Michael Myers kills Lynda and listens to Laurie through the receiver.

According to leading folklorist, Dr. Jan Harold Brunvand, this legend's origins trace back to about 1964 and have been reported throughout the continent as far north as Montreal, Quebec and as far south as Austin, Texas. Teenagers in particular are familiar with this tale as executive producer Moustapha Akkad notes: "The word 'babysitter' clicked with me because every kid in America knows what the babysitter is." In other words, Haddonfield could be any suburban town in America.

The second urban legend is called the "Killer in the Back Seat." In the middle of the film, Annie attempts to drive to her boyfriend's place. Once she is inside her car, the Shape springs up from the backseat and murders her. This legend traces back to 1967 and, though no actual murder cases have been reported, folks still check the backseat before stepping into their automobile. The urban legends are central to the *Halloween* screenplay because of their simplicity. Folklorists and film critics may analyze each, but the main purpose of such tales is to frighten us by preying upon the fear of being unsafe in either a car or the comfort of a suburban home.

The final urban legend is a reference to supernatural folklore. This is demonstrated in the scene when Bob leaves Lynda in bed to get a beer and makes the mistake of opening the closet door. Michael Myers bolts out and kills the teen, a classic footnote to the boogeyman that hides in the closet. This confirmation also takes place earlier when school

Halloween II: Laurie Strode (Jamie Lee Curtis) is glammed up and alone in a hospital that begs for more activity.

children tease young Tommy Doyle (Brian Andrews), claiming that the boogeyman is coming to get him. As in folklore, the child sees the boogeyman in the shadows and warns the adult, in this case, babysitter Laurie Strode, only to be told that it is all part of an overactive imagination. The closet is also used a final time in the film's climax as Laurie makes a failed attempt to escape the Shape. This time the urban legend is reversed. It is the victim who is hiding in the closet, while the boogeyman is in the bedroom trying to break in.

Common urban legends have found their way into *Halloween*'s sequels with limited success. In *Halloween II*, as Laurie is being rolled into Haddonfield Memorial Hospital, an unfortunate trick-or-treater is admitted after biting into a piece of candy (or perhaps an apple), and winds up with a severe mouth wound lined with a razor blade. This urban legend in particular still impacts today's society as it did in 1978. Parents are annually advised to check their children's candy for possible tampering, yet folklorists and sociologists insist that reports of what Jan Harold Brunvand calls "Halloween sadists" are based more on fear than fact. One case when Halloween candy caused a child's death is most likely where the urban legend originated. It took place in Houston, Texas on Halloween in 1974. Ronald Clark O'Bryan slipped cyanide into his son's (Timothy O'Bryan) Pixie Stix candy. The crime is tragic, but is a far cry from where legions of madmen spread terror by poisoning the masses. The urban legend in this film works because it is synonymous with Halloween itself. Other urban legends in the sequels don't work. In *Halloween 4*, Michael Myers is hiding in the back seat of Depu-ty Logan's patrol car as he pulls into Sheriff Meeker's (Beau Starr) house in an attempt to protect young Jamie Lloyd (Danielle Harris.) The scene doesn't work because it illustrates the policeman's lack of intelligence. Halloween is supposed to be the most dangerous night of the year in Haddonfield. Police are supposed to be on edge, having heard of Myers's notorious reputation. Yet, the viewer is supposed to believe that a trained law enforcement officer didn't notice the killer in the backseat at any time, including when he was driving the cruiser. This is a contrast to the similar scene with Annie in the original *Halloween* because the windows were fogged up and she was only in the car for a few seconds before being murdered. Later, Deputy Logan notices that the cruiser's rear door is open and, though he looks somewhat mystified by

Halloween II: **An evil pumpkin and a vulnerable nurse... alone**

this (because he drives in the *frontseat*, you know), he shuts the door and doesn't give it a further thought.

Halloween: The Curse of Michael Myers repeats this urban legend when obnoxious D.J. Barry Simms (Leo Geter) is talking on the phone while entering his vehicle. By this time, however, the outcome is expected. Not only does a close-up of Simms's face appear, which suggests that something is approaching, but he insults Michael Myers before he dies. This seems to be an unofficial rule in horror films: Supporting characters can't slur the killer and live. Like the "Killer in the Backseat," another urban legend is repeated in *Halloween 5*. In the original *Halloween*, Michael "the Boogeyman" Myers attacks from the closet to kill the just-had-sex teen. In *Halloween 5*, Myers is hiding in the closet again as Rachel is picking out a sweater to wear. This scene doesn't work because it takes place in the well-lit afternoon and Michael Myers is standing in front of her as she scours through her clothes. The previous "boogeyman-in-the-closet" scenes could happen, which makes it scary. The latter scenario is too hard to believe, especially since Rachel was shown to be a smart heroine in *Halloween 4*.

Another technique that is taken for granted in the original *Halloween* is the lighting, or rather, the lack of lighting. When watching *Halloween*, no doubt exists in the viewer's mind that the night scenes were indeed shot at night. Carpenter used just enough lighting and took full advantage of the darkness to make every scene work. The darkness also dominates all three main murders. No close-up occurs on the cord Michael Myers uses to strangle Annie. We don't see Lynda wriggling on the ground, watching her last breath. We also don't see the Shape's knife stab into Bob's chest. All of it is suggestive or covered in darkness. The darkness is also effective in the scenes where Tommy Doyle looks out the window and sees Michael Myers, either standing across the street as trick-or-treaters dash by, or, carrying Annie's corpse into the house. The shadows also dominate the climax inside the Doyle house from the time the Shape hides behind the couch to the close-up we see of him before Dr. Loomis empties his revolver. The darkness not only conceals a lot of potential gore that *Halloween* could have produced,

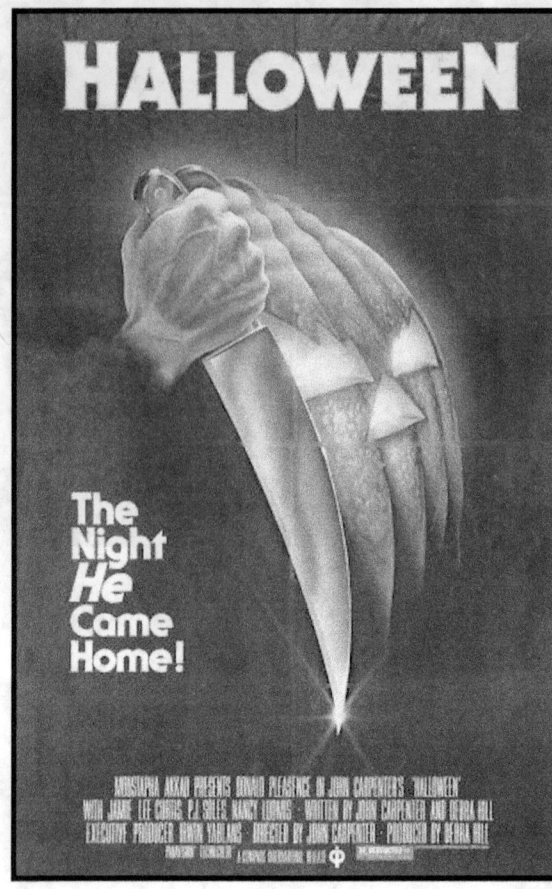

it fuels the suspense, forcing the viewer to fill in the blank spots on where everything (include the Shape himself) could be.

The lighting among many of the scenes in the sequels is inefficient. *Halloween II* did produce an effective scene where the lighting was just right. It involved candy striper Janet (Ana Alicia) discovering Dr. Mixter's (Ford Rainey) body. As she steps back in horror (why she didn't scream or gasp, we'll never know), the Shape's mask fades in from the black background directly behind her. Despite this effective scene, *Halloween II* lacks the original's ability to sneak up on the nervous viewer. Michael Myers's concentration shifts to murdering a hospital staff member instead of stalking Laurie Strode, but perhaps, just as importantly, he doesn't hide in the shadows anymore. He's out in the open, walking the streets and hospital hallways. *Halloween 4* also has one standout scene when it comes to the lighting. It's in the opening montage as the credits fade in and out. We see Halloween shots such as a paper skeleton stapled to a door, a scarecrow sitting on a tractor and sharp farm equipment. The background is a timber sky with traces of sea foam green. The montage not only makes the viewer shiver, even if watching it in July, but the montage captures the holiday's essence. The sounds of wind mixed with the subtle scary music is icing on the cake.

Unfortunately, *Halloween 4*'s lighting takes a nosedive after the introduction. Most scenes look like director Dwight Little attached a piece of blue film over the camera's lens and called "Action!" in the middle of the day. One can see a hint of blue light in almost every night scene, but two scenes best exemplify this. The first scene is when Michael Myers kills Bucky (Harlow Marks), the power plant worker, via electrocution. The second scene is when Michael Myers walks up the stairs in Sheriff Meeker's house and confronts Brady (Sasha Jensen), who is trying to load a shotgun. *Halloween: The Curse of Michael Myers'* director Joe Chappelle takes a similar approach when Jamie Lloyd (this time, J.C. Brandy) and her newborn make their escape in the opening scenes. Later, a shot occurs of the Shape walking out of his house and crossing the street to kill Kara Strode (Marianne Hagen) and her son Danny (Devin Gardner). We notice that cobalt blue lights dominate the sets in an attempt to give the illusion that it is nighttime. The results are ironic: the higher the budget, the phonier the sets look. *Halloween 5* is even shoddier. The worst lighting takes place in the booth in the barn where sex between two teens goes awry, and the Myers' house, which went from being a quaint little lot to a huge Gothic mansion. Director Dominique Othenin-Girard doesn't even attempt to hide the white light that blazes through the boarded-up windows, even though the scenes are suppose to be taking place late at night.

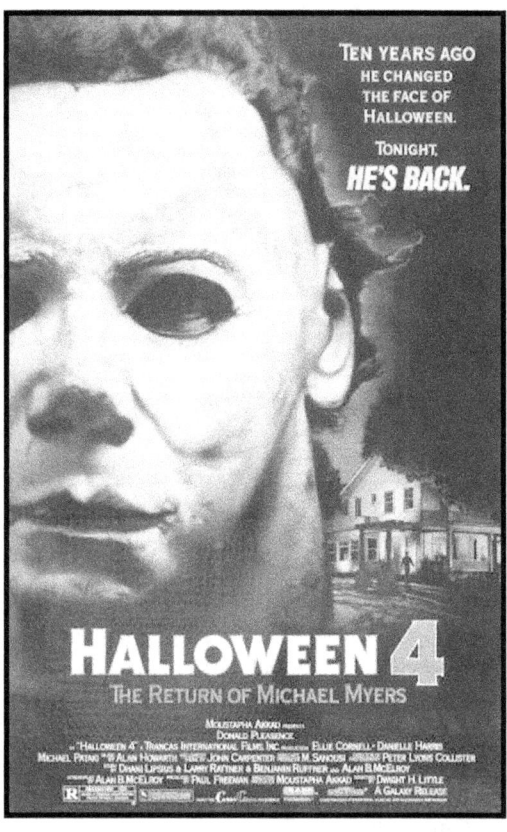

The last elements that flawed the series are obvious: inconsistency and lazy writing. Under most circumstances when writing a sequel, the author has an obligation to acknowledge the past while subtly incorporating his own style into the current project. I am aware that even the best writers never fully get the backstory just right and minor flaws can be excused. When choosing a suitable setting, however, the author should never insult the viewer's intelligence, which has often happened in this series.

Halloween 4 is a favorite among fans. The script is good yet blemished. Michael Myers murdering the entire police department seems like a cop out (no pun intended) and eliminates potential complexity. The film would have been stronger if officers were scouring the streets. Myers can also add impaling victims' brains with his thumb and stabbing victims with a shotgun to his list of creative but unconvincing murders.

In *Halloween 5*, Myers is suddenly wearing a new mask, even though the film takes place where part four left off. Perhaps he found his new mask with the ski-jump nose and overly huge neck in the mineshaft he fell down while Haddonfield's finest were lighting the dynamite. Escaping the brunt of the explosion, Myers falls into a very deep sleep. The town hermit watches over him until Myers wakes up, which is conveniently on Halloween Eve. Myers's niece, Jamie Lloyd, suddenly has a telepathic link with him, but that angle fizzles out and stabbing people is once again the script's prime objective. Dr. Loomis, who for years proclaimed Myers to be pure evil, suddenly wants to rehabilitate him: too many conveniences, not enough logic. In the end, a man in black breaks the Shape out of jail.

Halloween: The Curse of Michael Myers promised to answer some questions proposed in part five, but didn't. Myers kills Jamie Lloyd 15 minutes into the film so the

Halloween: Resurrection: **Is it The Shape, Michael Myers, or is this the jokster played by Busta Rhymes trying to scare the pretty young girls?**

next logical step is to pick on the closest thing to a relative—the Strodes, who conveniently (there's that word again) live in the old Myers house. Everyone in Haddonfield seems to know this fun fact except the Strode kids. Not that it matters. Most of the characters are killed off while we listen to a modernized, overdone, faced-paced and annoying *Halloween* theme song that drowns out John Carpenter's simple but creepy chords. We discover that the man in black (Mitchell Ryan) from *Part Five* is the leader of a devilish Druid cult that wants to use the Shape's evil for some unspecific reason: Another angle that goes nowhere. The cult members die and the surviving characters are never heard from again, including Donald Pleasence's Dr. Loomis. Unfortunately, Pleasence passed away during post-production, leaving a void that will never be filled in future installments.

Here are some other examples of lazy script writing:

In *Halloween II:*

Much of this movie takes place in Haddonfield Memorial Hospital. A reasonable choice considering that it begins right where the original left off. The question is, how come only a handful of staff members and no visible patients appear in such a gigantic building?

Nurse Karen (Pamela Susan Shoop) is already in danger of being fired, yet the threat of losing her job doesn't stop her from getting in a hot tub with her paramedic boyfriend. That would have been quite a black mark on her resume…if she had survived, of course.

Why exactly did Michael Myers break into the schoolhouse and why write "Samhain" on the blackboard? Another angle lost in limbo.

When Loomis discovers the link between Laurie and Michael Myers, why didn't he force the State Marshall to order backup on the CB *before* entering the hospital?

In *Halloween 4: The Return of Michael Myers*:

In the beginning of the film, Michael Myers' head is bandaged up. Why? Surely, the burns he received in *Halloween II* have healed after 10 years. The reason is probably because the filmmakers didn't want the viewer to see his face, but bandages aren't necessary. Creative camera angles, perhaps one from the Shape's view, could have avoided this. To top it all off, how is he suppose to breathe?

The Shape is somehow able to track down his niece's residence, which is listed under her stepparents' name, in record time. We never know how he came to such conclusions.

Throughout the film, Jamie Lloyd is running for her life from her evil uncle and, yet at the end, she is compelled to hold his hand while he lays unconscious.

Rachel falls off a roof and yet regains consciousness in time to know that her niece was in the local schoolhouse and opts to go after her, unarmed and unassisted.

In *Halloween 5: The Revenge of Michael Myers*:

Jamie Lloyd's entire stepfamily has left her for an out-of-town commitment on the anniversary of one of the most tragic nights of her life. One would think Rachel, Mr. Coruthers or Mrs. Coruthers would say, "Hey, why don't you come with us? After all, you have been getting death threats."

Once the cavalry arrives, the logical step is to take Jamie to safety and call for backup. Instead, they take Jamie to her uncle's house and use her as bait to lure Myers into a trap. Then, all but one cruiser abandons the plan and exits from the Myers house at the first sighting tip they get.

In *Halloween: The Curse of Michael Myers*:

The Strodes, living in Myers' house, have Halloween decorations all over their yard. This doesn't fit with the overacting and crabby John Strode who appears to hate everything about Halloween. The character uses an axe to chop down a cardboard figure of the Shape that is embedded on a pole—a kid's prank. It would be logical for John Strode to pull the pole out of the ground, but then if he did, Michael Myers wouldn't later have a weapon.

The Shape is able to place Barry Simms's corpse in a tree, located in the middle of Town Square, among the trick-or-treaters, without anyone noticing. Wait, it gets better. We are also supposed to believe that a child is stupid enough not to notice the body or that she is being trickled in blood. "It's raining red," the child says.

The climax takes place in Smith's Grove Sanitarium. According to Dr. Loomis in *Halloween 4*, the distance between Haddonfield and Smith's Grove is a four-hour drive, yet in this film, it feels like it is just around the corner. As with Haddonfield Memorial Hospital, this large building appears empty of staff and patients.

Issue 76

Barry Simms tells Tim Strode (Keith Bogart) and his girlfriend Beth (Mariah O'Brien) that he will meet them at the Myers house in five minutes, to do a live broadcast. So what do Tim and Beth do once they arrive, knowing that Barry Simms will be there any minute? They have sex (and not even a quickie) and Tim takes a shower.

Tommy Doyle (this time, Paul Rudd) lives with a senile old woman named Mrs. Blankenship (Janice Knickrehm). Although he is able to develop his "Thorn theory," he wasn't able to discover that the old lady he lives with is part of the Thorn Club.

In *Halloween: H20*:

In the prologue, Marion's house is broken into. She runs next door to call the police. Even though there could be a dangerous felon lurking in Marion's house, the neighbor has no problem entering it armed with only a hockey stick. When this unpersuasive scene takes place, daylight can be seen. Five minutes later, Jimmy comes out of the house and it is suddenly dark.

Laurie Strode seems to have forgotten that she had a daughter, nor does it seem that anyone in either Langdon, Illinois or Summer Glen, California has heard that Michael Myers struck Haddonfield in 1988, 1989 and 1996.

In *Halloween: Resurrection*, Michael Myers and a paramedic switch places. This leads to Laurie Strode chopping off the paramedic's head in *H20*'s conclusion. Although the paramedic's arms are free, it doesn't occur to him to take the mask off before she winds up her axe.

After *Halloween: The Curse of Michael Myers* bombed, Dimen-sion Films realized that they needed help with the series much like the way the Titanic needed more life-boats. Enter Kevin Williamson, whom many believe saved the horror franchise in the 1990s with his creative script, *Scream,* and paved the way for "smarter, non-clichéd slasher films" (which is ironic because such imitations like *I Know What You Did Last Sum-mer, Valentine* and *Urban Legend* were not smart or non-cliché, but that's another article). Williamson does the outline, Dimension hires a respected director named Steve

Miner and thank God Jamie Lee Curtis is back as Laurie Strode. *Halloween H20* (which sounds more like a movie about chemistry than a killer) is a hit and rightfully so. Although it has its errors, the film is arguably the smartest of the series. The opening credits are an excellent tribute to Donald Pleasence and his character. The script is more about showing what becomes of Laurie Strode after her traumatic night in 1978 rather than knifing people. The climax is respectable and Michael Myers is finally killed. The series ends on a high note.

What's that? *Halloween H20* is a hit? "Well let's make another one!" producer Moustapha Akkad says. The result is *Halloween: Resurrection*, which doesn't live up to its name.

For those who are still ardent fans of this series, this article will end on a good note. Yes, there is hope. Different roads potentially exist that Dimension Films haven't gone down yet. One of the better ideas is based on the *Halloween* comic book written by Phil Nutman and Daniel Farrands. The premise is a younger Dr. Loomis chronicling Michael Myers' boyhood years in Smith's Grove Sanitarium. Another halfway decent idea that was considered was *Helloween*. With the success of New Line Cinema's *Freddy vs. Jason*, Dimension Films brainstormed a crossover film of their own in which Michael Myers fights *Hellraiser's* Pinhead. This idea was voted against in a recent online poll at Horror.com, but if the film were conceived, it would likely jumpstart both waning franchises. Dimension Films has also approached New Line Cinema for a possible three-way dance in the probably inevitable *Freddy vs. Jason* sequel. A final proposal is to convince Jamie Lee Curtis and John Carpenter to reunite and give this series a suitable finale. Don't hold your breath on this one either. Jamie Lee Curtis has moved on to greener pastures and John Carpenter has distanced himself from his creation for over 25 years, having no desire to film the same kind of movie over again (although such a philosophy didn't apply to *Escape from L.A.*).

Halloween fans can't help but want a sense of closure. Rob Zombie's remake of the original *Halloween* failed to jumpstart the franchise. For every Donald Pleasence, there are a hundred Busta Rhymes, ready to drag the series into the purgatory of mediocrity, or even bad, moviemaking. All this makes the John Carpenter original seem ever more of a classic as the years pass.

JAMIE LEE CURTIS AND THE VIRGINITY MYTH

by Mark Allan Gunnells

Some actresses are known as Academy Award winners; others are known for their sex appeal; still others are known as character actresses who disappear completely into each role. Jamie Lee Curtis is known as the ultimate modern Scream Queen. Sure, in the 30 years since Curtis first started acting, she has found success in a wide variety of dramatic and comedic roles, but for some of us, she will be best remembered for a string of horror films she starred in, at the beginning of her career. In the late 1970s and 1980s, in only a handful of films made over a period of less than five years, Curtis made an indelible mark on the horror film genre, creating a legacy to which every young horror film actress since has aspired. Over the course of her career, Curtis has not always been comfortable with her status as a cinematic Scream Queen, but her contribution is undeniable. This status was further cemented with the 1996 release of Wes Craven's mega-hit *Scream*. In that film, several Jamie Lee Curtis references are made, and scenes from her screen debut, *Halloween*, are featured prominently in the climax. One character even speculates that the reason Curtis was the survivor of all her horror films was because she always played the shy virginal character.

And there it is, the common misperception that Curtis *always* portrayed the virgin, the one whose very sexual inexperience makes her somehow capable of outsmarting the killer in the end. Long before *Scream*, Curtis had this reputation, suggesting that she had been typecast in her horror work. However, this reputation is unfounded. While in her most famous role as Laurie Strode in *Halloween*, Curtis did in fact play a shy virginal character that survived while her sexually active friends were massacred. This is actually the only time she ever played such a character. In subsequent films, Curtis showed a greater range than she is often credited for essaying, creating disparate young women who in some ways mirrored the changing roles of women in society at the time.

When discussion of Curtis' contribution to the genre arises, 1978's *Halloween* is the film that is typically the primary focus of attention. After all, it was this film that

Jamie Lee Curtis as Laurie, the virginal babysitter, from the original *Halloween*.

made Curtis a star. Three years later, she reprised her role in the Carpenter/Hill-scripted *Halloween II*, a substandard sequel directed by Rick Rosenthal. Twenty years after the original, Curtis returned in Steve Miner's surprisingly effective *Halloween H20*, and she closed out the Laurie Strode storyline in 2002's let's-close-our-eyes-and-forget-it-ever-happened *Halloween Resurrection*, again directed by Rosenthal. The *Halloween* series has become one of Hollywood's most successful horror franchises, and the original has gone down in history as the standard by which all slasher films are judged.

And yet I'm not going to spend too much time on the *Halloween* films. They have been discussed *ad nauseam* over the years. Instead, I want to focus my discussion on the other three horror films in Curtis' oeuvre. These films—*The Fog* (1979), *Terror Train* (1980) and *Prom Night* (1980)—rarely get the attention that *Halloween* garners, and that is one of the reasons why the misperception of Curtis always playing the virginal character persists after all this time. I want to look at each film individually, examine the roles played by Curtis and illustrate how these characters offer a glimpse into the lives of real women during the time period the films were made. The object here is to prove that Curtis is more than a one-trick pony.

After the unprecedented success of *Halloween*—which became the highest grossing independent film of its time—director John Carpenter followed that classic with a story of ghostly retribution called *The Fog*. Curtis was cast as free-spirited hitchhiker Elizabeth Solley. She was not the star of the film, as the movie boasted an ensemble cast of both relative newcomers and seasoned pros. Curtis' own mother, Janet Leigh of *Psycho* fame, also had a prominent role, although mother and daughter did not interact directly onscreen. The film also starred sex-pot Andrienne Barbeau as disc jockey Stevie Wayne, a role that actually downplayed her physical assets and allowed her to play a more realistic, down-to-earth character, something she would rarely get to do in the years to come.

While Barbeau's sexuality is tempered in the film, Curtis' is actually ratcheted up a notch. The audience is first introduced to her character when she thumbs a ride from Nick Castle, played ably by Tom Atkins. After a shared beer and some banal chitchat,

Laurie Strode, innocent, demonstrates her will to survive during the climax of *Halloween*, as she confronts Michael Myers alone.

the two end up at Castle's place and have sex. Only afterward does Curtis' character get the name of the gentleman with whom she has just shared a bed, and only when he offers it; she never asks—quite a different character than awkward, inexperienced Laurie Strode.

In fact, it is a testament to Curtis' ability as an actress that the two roles are so drastically dissimilar and yet both so convincing. As Laurie Strode, Curtis captures the insecurity and social ineptitude of the character perfectly, infusing the role with warmth and naiveté. When Laurie discusses, with her friend Annie (Nancy Loomis, also costar of *The Fog*), her desire to go to the school dance, audiences easily see her inability to work up the courage to ask anyone to go with her, thus demonstrating a palpable and real yearning in her character. Curtis embodies the character so naturally that the audience finds suspension-of-disbelief effortless.

Curtis does such a stellar job portraying Laurie Strode that one would expect audiences to have difficulty accepting her as a character as different as Elizabeth Solley, and yet the actress proves more than up to the challenge. Whereas Laurie is mousy and timid, Elizabeth is bold and brazen. Curtis suggests a kind of easy sensuality, not through provocative clothing or comedic double entendres, the tools of lesser actresses, but simply with her attitude. She doesn't overdo her performance, but projects with ease a confidence and daring that is the polar opposite of Laurie Strode, but no less compelling or credible. Elizabeth Solley is not shy and certainly no virgin, and yet Curtis plays her to perfection.

When *The Fog* was initially released, reaction to the film was not over-whelmingly positive. Many people compared the movie to *Halloween* and found it lacking. The box office was rather disappointing in comparison to the previous Carpenter/Curtis outing, and the film was considered something of a failure. However, time has been kind to *The Fog*. Distance has allowed mainstream critics to judge the movie based on its own merits, and consensus seems to be that the film is flawed yet competent. It has achieved a cult status over the years and is now generally considered an effective ghost story. In

Nick Castle (Tom Atkins) and hitchhiker Elizabeth Solley (Jamie Lee Curtis) are strangers who share a bed in *The Fog*.

2005, an unfortunate remake was released that served only to accentuate the strengths of the original. While *The Fog* was not as influential to the genre as *Halloween*, it did prove that Carpenter had more to offer as a director, showing that he could do different types of films effectively. It also proved that Curtis had range as an actress. Although both films fall into the category of horror, Curtis portrayed two characters that were nothing alike, and she made the audience believe in the authenticity of both.

In some ways, the character of Elizabeth Solley was a more realistic representation of women in the late '70s than was Laurie Strode. The women's liberation movement was well underway by this time, and women were beginning to embrace and assert their own power. The age of the timid, obedient woman who did what she was told and had no mind of her own was long gone, if it ever truly existed in the first place. Women were taking charge of their own fates and setting their own courses through the world, no longer looking toward men to give their lives meaning or direction.

One of the many ways this new attitude manifested itself among women in the late '70s was through a newfound sexual aggressiveness that would have been unthinkable to women of past decades. The myth that men were the only ones with strong libidos had been debunked, and women were reveling in the pleasures of the flesh as well. The women of the '70s were not waiting around for men to make the first move; they were making moves and advances of their own. In the pre-AIDS world, a sexual freedom existed that everyone—women and men alike—was celebrating, throwing off the chains of Puritanism and repression in favor of sexual frankness and exploration.

Within a genre that has often been accused of espousing traditionally moralistic and misogynistic values—bad girls who have sex with their boyfriends get killed while good girls who abstain survive—the character of Elizabeth Solley flies in the face of such ideas. Here is a woman whose confidence and comfort with her own sexuality reflects what was going on in society at the time, and she is portrayed not as a bad girl in need of punishment but as a fully realized three-dimensional character. Her sexuality does not

Jamie Lee Curtis, as she appears in *The Fog*, becomes a more hard-edged character, less innocence and softness.

define her or condemn her but becomes a natural part of who she is. While I am not suggesting either Carpenter or Curtis was attempting to make such a statement with the film or the character, Elizabeth Solley in *The Fog* does in fact show that Curtis was capable of playing more than the virgin and that she had the talent to portray women of varying types realistically.

After acting in two Carpenter films back-to-back, Curtis moved on to director Roger Spottiswoode's *Terror Train*. This is perhaps the least remembered of Curtis' early horror work. The film takes the standard slasher formula and places it on a moving train during a New Year's Eve masquerade ball thrown by a bunch of college seniors. More so than Curtis' previous films, *Terror Train* operates as a mystery as well as a horror film, complete with an ending that most audiences find as surprising as *The Sixth Sense* or *The Crying Game*. The film, while not necessarily breaking new ground in the genre, has a stylish look and boasts some impressive performances.

Curtis plays Alana Maxwell, a young college student with a promising future, plenty of close friends and a steady boyfriend who wants to marry her. Again, Curtis is cast in a role that is nothing like Laurie Strode, but neither is the character like Elizabeth Solley. Alana and Elizabeth both share self-assuredness, and the suggestion seems to be that Alana is sexually active, but Alana is not the wild child that Elizabeth is.

While Alana is not portrayed as being shy or virginal, she is committed to her boyfriend Mo (Timothy Webber). She does engage in some flirtatious behavior with a magician hired to work the party (played by none other than David Copperfield), but she comes across as strictly a one-man woman. She illustrates that sex and morality are not mutually exclusive, that a person can be virtuous without being a saint.

Also, Alana seems more focused and goal-oriented than Elizabeth. Curtis' character in *The Fog* was a drifter, hitching her way across country while she worked on her art; Alana is a college girl with big dreams of a career in medicine. While the character is outgoing and popular, she is also dedicated to academics and serious about school. In some ways, Alana seems a mixture of the best attributes of Laurie and Elizabeth, incorporating both the former's studiousness and the latter's confidence.

Curtis' character in *Terror Train* is not easily intimidated. The one time that she does give in to peer pressure and participates in a cruel prank, disastrous consequences result, but she is the only one in the group to show any genuine remorse. She is quick to stand up to her boyfriend's obnoxious best friend Doc (Hart Bochner) and put him in his place whenever he is acting like a jerk, which is quite often. She also doesn't give in to the pressure being put on her to quit school and marry her boyfriend. Her best friend Mitchy (Sandee Currie) tries to convince her to do just that, but Alana never wavers in her conviction that she is doing the right thing by placing her education above all else. While it seems obvious she loves Mo, it is also obvious that she is an independent woman who is not looking for a man to support her.

Terror Train allows Curtis the opportunity to play a more diverse range of emotions than in her previous films. She isn't just being terrorized here but is going through many different emotional states. She is consumed with guilt over the ill-conceived prank, she is angry with Doc for the way he manipulates people and she is grieving for the deaths of her friends. It is a much more complex character than she has played before, and again, she manages to pull it off with aplomb. There isn't a false note in her performance; every action and nuance is genuine.

Just as Curtis' character in *The Fog* represented the sexual freedom that women of that time were experiencing, the character of Alana also offered a glimpse into women in the new decade of the 1980s. Women were not only starting to recognize their power sexually but also intellectually and professionally. Women were entering the workforce in record numbers and moving up the corporate ladder with greater speed and success. The days of Betty Homemaker may not have been completely over, but Sally Businesswoman was becoming more prominent in society.

Only a few decades prior, the traditional view was that women were to be housewives and mothers. The men were to go out into the workplace and earn the money, and the women were to stay home and handle the cooking, cleaning and child rearing.

Women in the workforce were rare, and women in positions of power were even harder to find. It may seem somewhat barbaric to a modern sensibility, but once such views were commonplace in this society, accepted by both men and women alike. Rarely did anyone upset the status quo.

But by the 1980s, the status quo had been irrevocably altered. Women were becoming serious about their education and their subsequent careers. It was no longer just assumed that a woman would find a nice man, marry, bear his children and then dedicate her life to her family. Many women no longer found the idea of that kind of life appealing or satisfying; they wanted more.

There was resistance to this movement, from women as well as men. Some people continued to view the woman's place as in the home, and women with ambition were often criticized and encouraged to give up their dreams and career goals in favor of a simple life of marriage and children. However, the tide had changed. Women were embracing the business world, expanding their minds and pursuing their dreams. Occupations that had once been male-dominated were now seeing females in the ranks, and women were ascending to top positions in companies and corporations.

Although this aspect of Curtis' character is not a vital component to the plot of *Terror Train*, I believe its inclusion adds an extra level of verisimilitude that makes Alana both more believable and a stronger character overall. With just a few exchanges of dialogue that could easily have been overlooked by mainstream audiences, Alana is established as a true woman of the '80s, determined and smart, self-reliant and ambitious.

After having played a college senior, Curtis next reverted back to playing a high school senior in Paul Lynch's underrated *Prom Night*. She was cast as Kim Hammond, a popular high school student voted Prom Queen by her class, a young woman still mourning the death of her younger sister six years prior. While she doesn't realize that three of her friends and her boyfriend were partially responsible for her sister's death, someone knows and is stalking the guilty teens on prom night.

The plot does not seem to deviate from the typical slasher fare, and most critics have dismissed the film as having nothing new to offer, but in some ways *Prom Night* actually defies the conventions of the genre. The film does contain the clichéd, awkward, virginal young woman in the character of Kelly (Marybeth Rubens), but instead of making the virgin the survivor, Kelly is actually the first character killed. In fact, she has her throat slashed almost immediately following her decision not to have sex with her boyfriend. So much for the rules of the horror film put forth by *Scream*.

Another way that the film is somewhat different from others of its ilk is that the main character, Curtis' Kim, is never in any direct danger from the killer. Since she is not one of the characters who harbors the dark secret of the girl's death, she is not a target. Her friends are stalked and picked off one by one, but she is never truly in the line of fire until she attempts to protect her boyfriend Nick (Casey Stevens), at the end of the film.

This leads to the final and perhaps most interesting way this film differs from most other slasher films. At the end of *Prom Night*, after the masked killer has murdered Kim's three girlfriends, he comes after Nick just as Nick and Kim are about to be crowned Prom King and Queen. Kim, seeing her boyfriend struggling for his life, joins the fight. She does what she can to save the man she loves, and in the end she bests the killer with his own axe.

In a typical slasher film, the woman is usually the one whose life is jeopardized and the big strong man must come to her rescue. It is even true of the first two *Halloween* films. While Curtis' Laurie does fight Michael Myers, in both the first film and its sequel Dr. Loomis (Donald Pleasence) saves her in the end. With *Prom Night*, the gender roles are reversed. Nick is cast in the traditional damsel in distress role, while Kim is the knight in shining armor who comes to his aid in his time of peril. It is a bold choice on the part of the filmmakers, and one that is largely overlooked when the movie is discussed.

This role reversal reflects the way society's views of women as weak and helpless were changing during the time the film was made. Women, often referred to as the weaker sex, had long been considered as incompetent and less equipped to take care of themselves than men. It was a commonly held belief that women needed a protector to shield them from the harsh realities of life. By the early '80s, this attitude was beginning to change, however. Women were realizing that they did not have to be eternal victims. They could demand respect and defend themselves against the unfairness of life.

In both the business world and relationships, women were starting to take control, no longer demurring to men but trusting in their own capabilities to see them through whatever hardships life threw their way. Women could even be heroes. The police force, firefighters, even the military—careers in which women were once considered too weak to excel—were seeing greater numbers of women taking on the challenge. The old gender barriers were being torn down, albeit reluctantly, and women were proving that they could be just as strong and courageous as men.

Curtis' Kim, while seemingly a typical character in a standard slasher film, is actually a subtle indicator of changing times. She is a symbol of bravery and female empowerment. She can in no way be considered a victim, and she is willing to put her own life on the line to save her man. She proves that women can be the heroes of their own lives, as well as horror films, and that men aren't the only ones who can wield the axe, so to speak. A less talented actress may not have been able to pack so much into this role, but Curtis' determination and strength shine through every word of dialogue and every gesture. In fact, Curtis' final scene with the killer contains some of the best acting I've personally ever seen in a horror film.

After completing *Terror Train*, Curtis closed out this particular chapter of her career by returning to the virginal character that had started it all. *Halloween II* picks up immediately where the original left off and has Laurie, wearing a ridiculous, unconvincing wig, being stalked by Michael Myers in an unrealistically abandoned hospital. While the setting of the hospital is inspired and creepy, the film makes a mistake in limiting Curtis' role. Laurie spends the majority of the film in a drugged stupor and shows none of the warmth or personality that made the character so appealing.

Following these five horror films, Curtis actively avoided the horror film genre for many years. After breaking into mainstream films, she went on to have a successful career in movies as varied as *Trading Places* (1983), *A Fish Called Wanda* (1988), *Blue Steel* (1990), *My Girl* (1991), *True Lies* (1994) and *Freaky Friday* (2003). In 1998, to commemorate the 20th anniversary of both *Halloween*'s release and Curtis' career in film, she decided to revive the role of Laurie Strode, the archetypal virgin that set the standard for such characters. *Halloween H20* finds Laurie Strode much changed from the sweet, shy girl audiences remember, right down to a fake name to hide her identity. Laurie is no longer that socially inept virgin, but over the years has become a fierce career woman raising a son on her own and turning to alcohol in an attempt to dull the pain of her traumatic past. Curtis delivers a powerhouse performance and shows that even shy virginal characters can grow up to be women with backbones of steel.

Due to a contractual obligation, Curtis returned a final time as Laurie Strode in *Halloween: Resurrection*. Her appearance in the film is brief, amounting to little more than an extended cameo. Here Laurie is reinterpreted as weary and a little mad, and the film ultimately rewards her years of perseverance with an unsatisfying end.

These days, Curtis is a woman who has aged gracefully and naturally, quite an oddity in youth-obsessed Hollywood, and she has said that she plans to retire from films. This is sad news to the movie industry indeed, but Curtis' legacy is firmly in place and will not soon be forgotten. And for horror aficionados, we will always be ready to bow before the ultimate Scream Queen.

My hope is that when her legacy is examined in years to come, people will recognize her contribution as more than just playing the virgin in horror films and celebrate the depth and complexity she brought to a wide variety of characters. Laurie Strode, Elizabeth Solley, Alana Maxwell, Kim Hammond—these are four very different young women, and yet Curtis managed to inhabit each of their skins in a way that was seamless. Much more than simply entertaining, Curtis' work in these horror films offered a peek into women's place in society in the late 1970s and early 1980s, exploring women's growing power over their own sexuality, their education and their careers. Jamie Lee Curtis has truly been the modern Every Woman, and every woman should feel proud to have had Curtis represent her.

WHY THE PLAN WORKS!
PLAN 9 FROM OUTER SPACE
by Carl Schultz

While I was cleaning out my attic recently, I found an old paperback compilation of *Son of Famous Monsters,* the softbound containing magazine articles from Forrest J Ackerman's *Famous Monsters of Filmland* magazine.

One of the articles was a feature about the movie *Plan 9 From Outer Space* published at around the time of the movie's original 1959 release, or shortly afterward.

It was fascinating to see what the movie's publicity coverage was like while *Plan 9* was still contemporary, and even more fascinating to see the movie treated with a modicum of respect. *Plan 9 from Outer Space* sure hasn't gotten much respect over the years. Generally it's referred to as the worst movie ever made—when it's referred to at all. It must be tough to live with a designation like that.

But speaking for myself, I changed my opinion of *Plan 9* a while ago, under some unusual circumstances. It was then I understood exactly why the plan worked.

Four or five years ago I was out of town on a trip, at a hotel in a city far away from home. One night I was feeling pretty lonely and isolated, unable to sleep although it was very late at night. So I took a walk to the lobby of the hotel to get myself a Coke and a smoke. Remember, this was the middle of the night.

Passing by one of the convention rooms off the main lobby, I heard laughter, cheers and some applause. I wondered what kind of meeting or reception could possibly be taking place at close to 3:00 a.m. in the morning. When I asked about the commotion at the registration desk, the night manager told me a film convention was going on at the hotel that weekend, and that the late show had just started in that particular room.

Somehow the phrase "the late, late show" struck a pleasant note in my memory. With 24-hour television programming, little room exists anymore for a late, late show. At one time almost every city with a television station had one. It came on at least once a week, usually on Saturday nights, and would feature an old movie—generally of the lousy variety—interrupted frequently by commercial advertisements for businesses both local and national.

Sam's Furniture of Phillipsburg, *Pee-Yay* had a great commercial on Altoona's Late, Late Show on WFBG—politically incorrect as all get out when you think about it—featuring three cardboard puppets dressed as Mexicans, playing guitars and singing the Sam's Furniture jingle to the tune of "La Campasita." I still sometimes catch myself whistling that little tune and thinking of those puppets.

And Ed Eisenhower, the host of KDKA in Pittsburgh's version of the Late, Late Show, would shamelessly hawk the Sealy mattresses available at the Kelly and Cohen's Department Store. At the end of the show, he'd kick his bedroom slippers off so hard that the slippers would fly up into the air over his head. Then he'd jump onto the Sealy bed and pretend to go to sleep.

The Late, Late Show would usually precede a pre-recorded prayer—sometimes called *Sermonette*—to conclude that day's television broadcast. The playing of The National Anthem would follow a television test pattern and then the hiss of dead air would continue until early morning. It was like your television's way of putting on pajamas, saying goodnight and climbing into bed.

Anyway, I wandered over to the convention room at the hotel that night and listened in for a moment, then opened the door and stepped inside. As my eyes adjusted to the

darkness, I realized that the room was large and filled with rows and rows of collapsible chairs. Mesmerized people filled most of these chairs and they were enraptured watching a scratchy 16mm print of *Plan 9 From Outer Space*.

Some people standing near the door looked like they were in charge of things, and I asked them if it would be okay for me to stick around and watch the movie for a couple of minutes. They shrugged and invited me to stay and watch the whole thing if I liked.

So I found an empty chair and watched *Plan 9 From Outer Space* for the umpteenth time, with a room full of strangers in a hotel in a city far away from home. But in a way I suddenly felt closer to home than I'd felt in years.

Sometimes I think we're very spoiled as a society by being given too many choices. With 24/7 cable broadcasts, movie channels and pay tele-vision stations, having only one entertainment choice is rare, and that night the choice was a scratchy, faded print of a lousy old movie that nobody really wanted to see, not even when it first premiered at the local Bijou.

Early in my life existed a time when any movie on tele-vision after one o'clock in the morning was a good movie, it meant there was somebody else in the dark and silent night also awake and unable to sleep. And the commercials were the icing on the cake.

Finding that room full of people watching *Plan 9 From Outer Space* reminded me that people miss that. Knowing that there are other lonely souls out there gives us a sad sense of hope and longing that only people in the middle of the night can feel. Meeting them, and sharing some time in their company, was something extra-special.

Books have been written about Edward D. Wood, Jr., and how awful and unpolished—awkward—his movies are. And it's true that *Plan 9* is a terrible movie, but many terrible movies exist. And yeah, it's ineptly made, but I've thought about it many times since that night and my opinion is that the only real difference in style between *Plan 9* and, say, something like DeMille's 1956 version of *The Ten Commandments*—the movie ABC Television shows America each and every Easter—is that one of the movies had a tiny budget and no major stars and the other had the backing of a major studio and a cast of expensive megawatt Hollywood stars, both behind and in front of the camera.

But *Plan 9* has something that most movies—including many expensive and profitable movies —do not, never have and never will have: a spirit and a heart that's full of enthusiasm, joy and happiness.

Obviously made by people who clearly love movies, *Plan 9*, once or again, is like going back to your old high school and checking out that year's class play after having seen all the plays on Broadway, or like watching a group of small children staging a pageant, earnest and solemn in their efforts to appear grown-up.

And since seeing *Plan 9 From Outer Space* that night in a room full of strangers, I think of it as a comfort food movie, and sit down and watch it again from time to time. I watch it every time I feel alone, or left out or forgotten, or when I'm just feeling a need for a boost of enthusiasm and joy. I finally "get it"…I comprehend the plan.

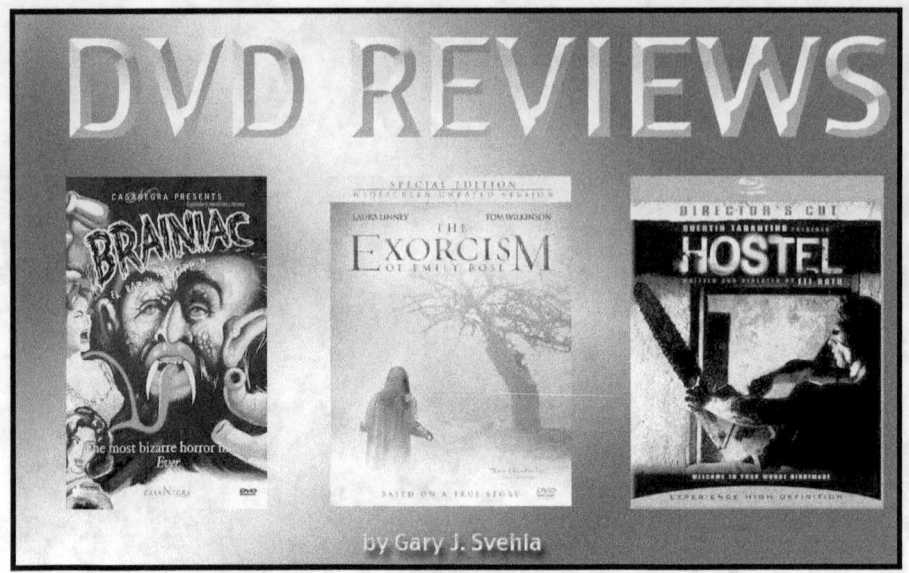

by Gary J. Svehla

Ratings:
4: Excellent; 3: Good; 2: Fair; 1: Poor

House of Wax
Movie: 2.0; Disc: 3.0
Warner

It's awfully deceitful to call this concoction *House of Wax*, for it is barely a remake of the 1953 classic starring Vincent Price (that 1953 movie itself a remake of *Mystery of the Wax Museum*, starring Lionel Atwill, made in 1932). This movie's spirit lies in the 1970s, and director Rob Zombie does the 1970s better than anyone working today. Actually, this movie could have been cleverer and called itself Houses of Wax or Waxing Poetically, although this tepid *House of Wax* contains very little visual poetry. Director Jaume Collet-Serra is sometimes interesting visually, but his entire approach to horror is to retread the past, and superior films such as Wrong Turn did this to better effect.

What is strong here is the cast of youthful offenders. The oddly sensual Elisha Cuthbert (the much maligned Kelly of TV's *24* and formerly a child actor who starred in Robert Tinnell's Air Speed and Believe), now remodeled as auburn and not blonde, is still perky and makes a fine heroine. She is joined by the current media sensation Paris Hilton, who is bland at best and hardly sexy. Her oddly ordinary face sits atop an elongated body that features long legs and big feet, and when she does her semi-striptease for her boyfriend, she barely sizzles. When Hilton is in danger, half-dressed and falling out of her night clothing, her bare-legs and barefeet thump her getaway. The more demure Cuthbert might wear short-shorts, but she also wears long wooly socks and sports a bloody mouth and lips, the end product of having the fiend Crazy Glue her lips shut. In the old slasher days the beautiful young heroine would flash her boobs seductively, but here Cuthbert strips off her tee shirt to reveal, from the back, a pretty bra as her army of male friends shield her exposure from the inbred hillbilly pervert. This ain't the 1970s! However the cast of characters (including Jared Padalecki from *The Gilmore Girls*) is well-defined and interesting performances abound. The first third of the script allows character development.

Yet the director makes some odd choices. The first victim is Padalecki, who is knocked on his butt when the wax-faced villain slashes the boy's Achilles' tendon. Soon the male is beaten and kicked into submission, drugged, stripped and strapped to a metal chair apparatus that is surrounded by tiny spray nozzles. The barely alive victim is coated with a spray of wax so he can be the next model in the town of wax corpses (similar to Dead and Buried, except here the corpses stay dead).

Director Collet-Serra creates two copycat villains that have long since become clichés. For instance, one of the villains is the good-old-boy psychopath, versed in the Bill Mosely school of acting. This is the typical over-the-top southern accented rant and raver with the knife. This guy, even when felled with two arrows from a crossbow, still survives to rip one of the arrows out of his arm. The other one, stuck in the chest, remains protruding only to be shoved further in during the bloody climax. Of course this freak has an even sicker brother, Vincent (hopefully not in tribute to Vincent Price), who wears a wax mask with one eye missing, and remains mute throughout the production. He becomes The Shape/Michael Meyers/Leatherface-style villain and projects the image of being just another walking nightmare with a sharp weapon. Together the brothers become horrifying figures as they mangle their victims after first torturing them into submission. But both performances and visualizations of villainy are rather old hat by now and thus lose much of their dramatic appeal. Collet-Serra has an obsession with feet—both serial lunatics slice the feet of more than one victim, but other than their mutilation of feet and spikes through the head, this director brings precious little originality to the table. The fiery explosive climax at *The House of Wax* is visually dazzling for several minutes, with gushing molten wax running everywhere and covering everything, but this is too little too late. This *House of Wax* is closer to cold snot than hot wax.

The Devil's Rejects
Movie: 3.0; Disc: 4.0
Lions Gate

Rob Zombie showed promise with his debut feature *House of 1,000 Corpses*, a film that sat on the shelf for over a year. Zombie's script was light on plot but heavy on ultra violence, punctuated with heavy metal music. It was a visceral film, an obvious homage to 1970s horror cinema, more a tribute than an original statement. Here, with a bigger budget, Zombie returns with the ultimate 1970s tribute, *The Devil's Rejects*, a film vastly superior to his debut. Once again we have our three social misfits forming the Firefly family: the sickly sensual Baby (Sheri Moon Zombie), her depraved father and perverse clown Captain Spaulding (Sid Haig) and the Charles Manson-eque Otis (Bill Moseley). Teaming together to tear 'em apart, the group's serial crimes are so ghastly and depraved that the media now calls them The Devil's Rejects.

First, the film's strength lies in its intense acting. Zombie, Haig and Moseley all submit lifelike performances of people we simply hate, sick puppies who have absolutely no redeeming qualities. When Baby is asked by one of her hostages if she can go to the bathroom, Baby smiles shyly and demands that the woman first do something for her. The request is for the terrified woman to slap her companion in the face as hard as she can. Only the third slap satisfies her, and only then does she allow the hostage to use the bathroom. But it is Zombie's perverse little-girl playfulness underlined with that sadistic streak, erupting violently, that defines her character. Sid Haig's rotten-toothed clown is defined by the sequence when he walks up to a mother and child and demands to have their car. When the mother defiantly tells the child to go into the car and lock the door, the look on Haig's face is classic, a who-the-f**k do you think you are type of disbelief, as the demanding but almost comical Captain Spauding comes to a slow boil and beats the woman, until she collapses on the ground. Spauding then speeds away in the car, but not before terrifying the young child until he lets him go. And the intense yet soft-spoken Bill Moseley's best sequence occurs when he declares himself Satan and beats Geoffrey Lewis to death with a wooden branch, repeatedly bashing his skull in while he shoots his second victim in the neck, and as Lewis lies bleeding to death on the ground, Mosely takes out his knife and carves the man's face off much in the style of Leatherface from Tobe Hopper's *Texas Chain Saw Massacre*.

These are miscreants of the most evil and violent nature, human fiends who can take a beating as well as dish it out. The trio is a family of criminals always harboring a hidden trick in order to survive (such as wearing body armor to lure the police into their farmhouse so these fiends can shoot the policemen to death while being protected from bullets themselves). Director Zombie includes a wonderful over-the-top performance by William Forsythe as obsessed Sheriff Wydell, who decides to take the law into his own hands to act out God's revenge for the death of his brother. And one hilarious sequence involves Wydell calling in a movie critic to decipher the meaning of the Firefly family using symbolic names (such as Captain Spaulding, a character role created by Groucho Marx). The pretentiousness of the self-confessed movie critic is very funny and adds a small slice of humor to an otherwise sick movie.

However well photographed (most 1970s horror films feature faded color and grainy cinematography, but not so *The Devil's Rejects*), edited, scored (instead of using modern heavy metal music, Zombie scores this movie with classic 1970s rock music which works beautifully) and acted, *The Devil's Rejects* panders to the most base of human desire and shows the audience serial crimes of the most intensely graphic nature. Perhaps the best sequence is the one where a rock band is held hostage in their hotel room. One of the band members suddenly gets shot point blank in the skull as a child screams and vomits in reaction. Next we have one woman forced to strip to her underwear as Otis explores her body with his pistol barrel. Another woman is found in the shower and forced onto the bed totally nude and vulnerable, to be not-so-playfully tormented. After everyone is brutally murdered, the lone surviving woman, found by a maid (who opens the apartment to clean but instead finds mayhem, blood and bodies in the bathroom) after the Rejects vacate the motel, runs out of the motel onto the highway, where she is promptly flattened by an 18-wheeler. The trail of blood and dismembered body littering the highway is truly sickening.

The Devil's Rejects is an exercise in depicting violent crime by well-defined criminals that somehow manage to hold our interest, much in the same way cars on the interstates slow down to rubber-neck accidents on the side of the road. Audiences feel guilty for enjoying such entertainment and the world of cinema might be a better place without such movies. However, when it comes to craft this movie might very well be among the best horror movie of the past few years. The DVD's second disc features a two-hour and 22-minute documentary on the making of the movie, which is superb, and the first disc features a slew of makeup tests, full commercials used from the movie, movie videos, deleted scenes, a gag reel, etc. Myself, I feel guilty as hell, but bottom line, *The Devil's Rejects* is intense and excellent moviemaking. Now, if Rob Zombie could only get the 1970s out of his system (do I need to refer to his recent and needless remake of *Halloween*?) and put his talent to something a little more original, he might yet become a director of renown.

Star Wars III: Revenge of the Sith
Movie: 3.0; Disc: 4.0
Fox

Revenge of the Sith, along with *Attack of the Clones*, is the best of the modern-day Star Wars trilogy, but it simply fails to rank artistically with any of the original

three entries. However technically these modern *Star Wars* films improved the use of special effects, their soulful magic is miniscule when compared to the original, cruder entries. The original three movies, even with their original effects, contained storytelling and characterizations that stand the test of time (especially the rogue Han Solo performance by Harrison Ford). Here the screen is often too busy with sensory bombardment that makes it difficult for the viewer to know where to focus. One generation after the birth of the original trilogy, even marvelous professionals such as Ewan McGregor, Natalie Portman and Samuel L. Jackson fail to resonate. In the new series it's the supporting players such as Ian McDiarmid (who was also great in *Return of the Jedi*) and Christopher Lee that stand out, not the feature players (though Alec Guinness proved this same theory true in the original trilogy). Unfortunately Hayden Christensen as Anakin Skywalker/Darth Vader is ultimately wooden and lacks the nuance to make his performance the classic one it deserves to be. Christensen's performance undermines any greatness the modern trilogy might project..

It seems that in the intervening years since *Return of the Jedi*, the final installment in the original trilogy, George Lucas has devoted himself to the technical side of filmmaking, neglecting storytelling and acting. While Lucas concocted all the *Star Wars* stories, in the original three he employed writing professionals such as Leigh Bracket and Lawrence Kasdan to craft the final screenplays (and Lucas only directed *A New Hope* himself), while Lucas both wrote the screenplays and directed all three new Star Wars entries. In other words, Lucas seems less the collaborator and more the DYI filmmaker, and the modern trilogy is worse off because of that ego-driven decision. Everyone understands that Star Wars will be Lucas' defining life's work and that he wanted his personal vision to be front and center. But film is a collaborative art and Lucas seems to have forgotten this. His instincts have not been as sharp this time around—the casting of bland child actor Jake Lloyd in *The Phantom Menace* and the commitment to creating and keeping Jar Jar Binks in all three movies (delightfully reduced to a quiet member of Padme's funeral procession in *Revenge of the Sith*) only demonstrates how one man's ego can lessen his artistic vision. Somehow the magic is undone.

Revenge of the Sith comes closest to recapturing the magic of the original three installments. Here the plot is heavily (and unsubtly) politically motivated, derived from that telling line of dialogue delivered by Padme, when she says so this is how democracy ends, with cheers and standing ovations. And even if Hayden Christensen's performance is not up to the task, his character as scripted is marvelous in its complexity, his dedication to the Republic so strong that he would even turn against the Jedi Knights, who are attempting to overthrow the Sith Lord Chancellor Palpatine (McDoirmid), Anakin's new master. Unwittingly helping Palpatine kill Jedi Master Mace Windu (Jackson), Anakin mutters sad indignation before swearing his allegiance to his new master, who represents the Dark Side of the Force (and this allegiance to the Dark Side is his only way to save Padme from death at childbirth). His obsessive love for his secret wife and his efforts to keep her alive allows him to sell his soul to the devil Palpatine and lose his humanity by becoming the semi-mechanical Darth Vader. The metaphor is not subtle, but it is startling nonetheless. The wondrous intercutting between Padme's birth sequence—and death—juxtaposed to the sequences where the legless and burned-beyond-recognition Anakin is reborn as Vader are the best sequences in the modern trilogy, and they contain the artistry and imagination woefully lacking in the three prequels. Here the emphasis is not on zooming spaceships or wondrous cityscapes, but on actual human drama that is character based, something Lucas lost sight of for most of the modern trilogy.

The drama of the slaughter and death of all the Jedi knights, even the children at the temple, is genocide at its worst. And the corruption and betrayal of Anakin makes the drama all the more horrible. Literally Obi-Wan and Yoda and a precious few remain to respond to the birth of the authoritarian Empire and the death of freedom and goodness in the universe. Even the death of Padme at childbirth and the birth of her new hope twins Leia and Luke cannot lessen the impact of utter defeat at the end of the dark tunnel of *Revenge of the Sith*. The movie is the darkest Star Wars of them all, and unlike all the other films that end on a note of hope, this third film ends with only a glimmer of hope derived from the birth of the twins and the final sequence where the children are lovingly given to their adoptive parents.

Revenge of the Sith resonates with emotion and the sense that this is the final episode ever of the *Star Wars* mythology, and as moviemaking goes, this film ends the series with a visceral punch (although the darkly lit lava and birth of Vader are again difficult to see as the screen is once again cluttered). The extra bonus disc is filled to the brim with goodies of all sorts, and it is heartwarming that Revenge of the Sith once again reminds viewers how classic these six films have become in our culture's collective consciousness. After the utter mediocrity of *The Phantom Menace*, it is important that the new trilogy ended on such a high (even if flawed) note.

One final thought. Having just viewed all six of the *Star Wars* films (in HD on HBO) in succession, even with their flaws, the modern trilogy makes the original trilogy resonate even more, adding history and faces to the mythology and making the victory at the conclusion of *Return of the Jedi* even more emotionally powerful. If we view those three modern *Star Wars* films as prelude to the dramatic opera of the original trilogy, why then the modern trilogy has done its job well enough. That is, setting the viewer up for the powerful three-film wallop of *A New Hope, The Empire Strikes Back* and *Return of the Jedi*. Together, all six films, after a slow build, produce one of cinema's most iconic and mythic works.

The Bird with the Crystal Plumage (Special Edition)
Movie: 3.0; Disc: 4.0
Blue Underground

It was way back in 1970 when writer-director Dario Argento debuted his thriller *The Bird with the Crystal Plumage*. Mario Bava, Argento's mentor, invented the giallo formula, but the subgenre was refined, transformed and ultimately defined by Argento. While Argento did much finer movies, *The Bird With the Crystal Plumage* was perversified Hitchcock, Euro-trashed and sexed up to the max. It was a movie of haunting visual style, yet at the same time it was violent and crossed the boundaries of what then constituted the thriller genre (although, again, Bava's similar thrillers in Europe transversed much the same territory).

Here is what Argento brought to the creative table so masterfully with this film. First, the atonal jazzy musical score, created by the master Ennio Morricone, established the sound of the giallo (it sounds cheesy after all these years to my ears). Secondly, and most importantly, Argento brought a lush visual sense to the thriller genre. His sequence where star Tony Mussante looks through the bright museum-front picture window (framed almost as a 16:9 movie screen, with bright light gushing forth into the Italian night) to see two shadowy figures struggle, a sexy well-dressed young woman and a man wearing a dark trenchcoat and hat, a knife flashing and plunging into the woman's stomach as the dark figure slinks away. The all-glass front is locked and Mussante is only able to look on in terror as the woman, now fallen and crying, crawls on her belly toward him, her bloody hand raised. The woman survives, but innocent Mussante is held for questioning, his passport taken from him.

Another plus Argento incorporated into his film was the surprise attack and flip-flop chase sequence where the cat first chases the mouse, but then the mouse ends up chasing the cat. For instance, in one spooky sequence the figure wearing the trench coat attacks Mussante on a moody night-lit street. Luckily the attacker's meat cleaver only chops a water pipe that gushes water, but the shadowy figure escapes. Soon a car runs down a policeman, who served as bodyguard to Mussante and his girlfriend. A Reggie Nalder-type figure emerges from that car, and he wears a bright yellow jacket. Armed with a silencer, the creepy hit man chases Mussante down a dark alley way and through a parking lot of 18-wheelers, Mussante able to remain one step ahead of his pursuer. Once he has escaped from the mysterious man in yellow, Mussante traces his attacker to a hotel. It seems the hotel is sponsoring a convention of former prizefighters, and every person in the room sports the same bright yellow jacket. So the fiend escapes into the night. Such dazzling visuals are variations on Alfred Hitchcock's trademarks, but in Argento's Italy a simple cityscape cat-and-mouse chase at night becomes totally unnerving and evil. Hitchcock conducted most of his chases by daylight with familiar settings accenting the action. Argento's world is defined by bright, glaring lights, dark parking lots, run-down buildings and tall walls. Nothing is familiar in Argento's visual world.

Another one of Argento's variations on a theme occurs when Mussante's girlfriend Suzy Kendall, alone in their locked hotel room, finds the fiend in the trenchcoat attempting to break into her room. The silent stalker uses a bright knife to bore a hole in the door, revealing his intense eye as he works to break through the other side after first cutting the phone cable and then the electricity. Kendall goes into hysterics and collapses on the floor, unable to help herself or do anything. Such a weak horror film heroine only reminds us that the era of the empowered woman remained almost seven years away. Her running around the apartment like a chicken with its head cut off, bolting one window, closing another one, increases the tension, but such silly shenanigans only seem ridiculous.

By the film's end a plot twist turns everything around and the actual murderer is portrayed as pure insanity with rolling eyeballs, twisted facial features and intense speech patterns. It's psychopath 101 cinema-by-the-numbers all the way. So while *The Bird with the Crystal Plumage* does feature a few sensational sequences (such as the shot of the man who falls to his death from the 10th story balcony of an apartment building, the camera following him all the way down), this movie more importantly defines the imaginative yet quirky director finding his unique vision and style. He is not altogether successful, but his first film suggests both mediocrity and vision and illustrates the initial vision of the man who would change the face of horror cinema during the 1970s and 1980s, and beyond. Extras include onscreen interviews with Argento, Morricone and the cinematographer Vittorio Storaro and actress Eva Renzi. An audio commentary track is also included. Blue Underground is picking up from where Anchor Bay left off; however, *The Bird with the Crystal Plumage* shows an artist straining to find his unique style.

The Val Lewton Horror Collection
Movies: *Cat People* (3.5); *Curse of the Cat People* (3.0);
I Walked with a Zombie (3.0); *The Body Snatcher* (3.0); *Isle of the Dead* (3.0);
Bedlam (2.5); *The Leopard Man* (3.5); *The Ghost Ship* (2.5); *The 7th Victim* (3.5);
Disc: 4.0
Warner

Even more so than the *Hammer Horror Collection* and *The Bela Lugosi Collection*, *The Val Lewton Horror Collection* deserves to be called the best horror film DVD release of the past few years, for it features every Val Lewton horror production restored to absolute brilliant picture and sound. Never have these films looked this dynamic, not even the laserdisc releases, which were pretty amazing. We can even compare the Criterion release of *Cat People* to the Warner Bros. release, and the Warner release is every bit as good.

1942's *Cat People*, inspired by Universal's *The Wolf Man*, is superior in every way, making up for loss of mood and detailed mythology with a more nuanced script, better performances and a more adult psycho/sexual underbelly. In fact *Cat People* is one of the greatest horror classics ever and deserves a spot in anyone's top-20. Jacques Tourneur's direction, DeWitt Bodeen's script, Nicholas Musuraca's cinematography and a marvelous cast of wonderful performers (especially Simon Simone's Irena) initiate a new era of adult horror movie filmmaking, produced at a modest cost. Even though female to panther transformations are suggested, and actual panthers are shown in Brownstone apartments, the emphasis here is psychological and physical monsters become secondary. The Lewton factory suggested horrors that dwell in our darkest nightmares, those very real fears that make individual lives overwhelmingly defective and prevent individuals from achieving happiness.

In his initial production, all the Val Lewton ingredients for horror are operational. The dank shadows that populate Lewton's world are not cast in mythological worlds of Varsaria but in then modern cities and realistic locales: the office, the zoo, apartment buildings, restaurants, etc. Lewton's horrors permeate the everyday world of the present. His hook for *Cat People* is a close investigation of a disintegrating marriage based upon fear of sex and intimacy. Irena, haunted by a Serbian curse that affected her village, believes that sexual arousal will cause her to turn into a panther. Living isolated and alone, the too-ordinary but good-looking Ollie (Kent Smith) falls in love with the

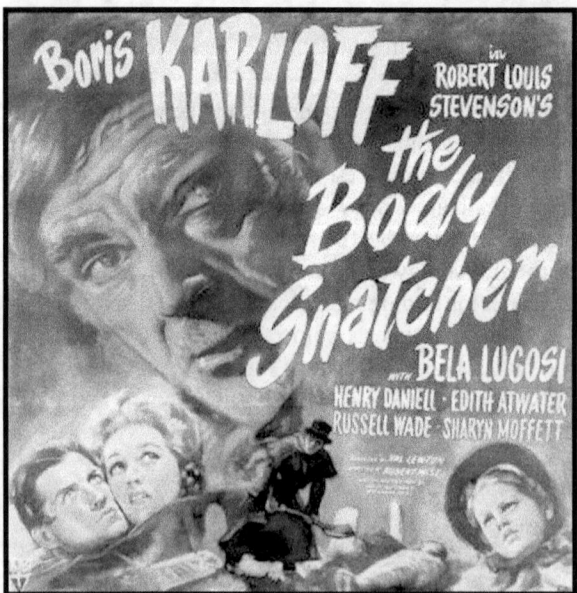

mesmerizing Irena and marries her. Even though the psychologically challenged virgin loves her husband and wishes to keep him happy, she barricades herself on the other side of the bedroom door, sits naked and shaking in the bathtub crying and stares outside her brownstone window looking at the falling snow, an absolutely perfect metaphor for her frigid mental and physical state. Only when the oily psychiatrist Dr. Judd (Tom Conway) tries to help Irena by seducing her, does she allow her passions to become aroused, turning into a beast and killing the doctor, but not before he spears her in the chest with his cane/sword, allowing the dying woman to confront the panther at the zoo one final time.

Seldom in B productions have such complex characterizations been drawn: the sexual yet frigid East European Irena, the dedicated to his work nuts-and-bolts Ollie and the "other woman," who works with Ollie, Alice (Jane Randolph). Whenever Ollie feels stressed or confused, he returns to the office where as an engineer he designs boats. There he seeks comfort from his confidante and best friend Jane, who slowly admits she has fallen in love with him. Ollie slowly comes to realize that his marriage with Irena will never be consummated and she will never satisfy his needs. Alice, while she is conniving and subtle, is basically a decent person, who hates to see the man she longs for suffer in a defective marriage. The subtle sequences of having the distraught Irena return home to find Alice there with Ollie only fuels the problems that destroy the marriage. Alice doesn't so much go after Ollie as allow herself to be around him whenever he needs emotional support. Seldom has a horror programmer probed the disintegration of a marriage in such detail, and in Lewton's world no actual villains exist, except for Dr. Judd, whose passion to help Irena might be even stronger than his lust for her.

It goes without saying that the script, the direction and the overall production all congeal to produce a horror movie that breaks new ground and demonstrates the formula for adult horror in the 1940s, and beyond. *Cat People* is a horror film classic and leaves the Unviersal monster rallies in the dust.

Curse of the Cat People, released in 1944, became director Robert Wise's first credit when he replaced the original director (although Gunther von Fritsch still receives co-director credit, even though most of his sequences were re-filmed). Once again the Lewton factory was given an exploitative title and had to build a movie around that title. After the success of *Cat People*, RKO expected a Universal-style sequel, but Lewton's creativity would never allow that. Screenwriter DeWitt Bodeen created a gentle child fantasy that used the ghostly Irena as playmate and confidante. Ollie, now married legitimately to Alice, is still depressed over the violent death of his former wife Irena and does not allow his daughter Amy to harbor any imaginative fancies, fearing that such illusions will overpower Amy's life much as it did Irena's. However, Amy (Ann Carter) seems to be more Irena's daughter than Alice's, and she lives in fantasy worlds of inner imagination. She is disappointed when none of the school kids attend her birthday party, but in her fantasy she mailed the invitations to her schoolmates by placing the letters in her magic mailbox tree in the backyard, where they remain. Of course all the kids at school taunt and avoid the child because of her strange ways.

But soon the light-hearted, child-oriented drama turns dark and spooky. Amy is fascinated by the local neighborhood witch house, a run-down home populated by an old retired actress, Mrs. Farren (Julia Dean), who suffers from dementia and lives with her witchy adult daughter Barbara (Elizabeth Russell). Barbara tries to frighten Amy from visiting her mother. What we have are two depictions of fantasy life, one, an innocent child's make-believe world that is harmless. But the second fantasy involves Mrs. Farren's denial that daughter Barbara is actually her daughter (Farren insists that her real daughter died) and this causes Barbara to turn bitter and despondent because all she wants is for her mother to acknowledge and love her. Farren's senility is a harmful fantasy that destroys her relationship with her daughter. Amy's fantasy is acceptable and healthy, but her father does not allow her the freedom to use her imagination in that manner. So *Curse of the Cat People* is actually about the clash of childhood fantasy vs. dementia/old age fantasy, demonstrating how the world of imagination is seldom tolerated in the modern world and how our loved ones feel threatened by such imaginative escapes from hardcore reality. By the movie's end Mrs. Farren comes to accept Barbara as her daughter (after the enraged daughter almost strangles Amy because of feelings of jealousy) and Irena announces she will now take her leave of Amy, allowing the child to confront the world of reality head on (although Irena believes Amy now has the strength to do so). Thus *Curse of the Cat People* is bittersweet, demonstrating how mother and daughter and father and daughter can only be emotionally reunited if sacrifices are made. While not quite a horror movie, *Curse of the Cat People* does have a harder emotional edge than most people give it credit. The movie deals quite realistically with the chasms that cause loving relationships to disintegrate, a similar theme from *Cat People* but here handled a little differently.

Jacques Tourneur's *I Walked With a Zombie*, to me, is the most overrated Val Lewton production, but many people claim it is the best. To be quite honest, *I Walked With a Zombie* contains several stellar moments: the ultimate Lewton "walk" of nurse Betsy Connell (Frances Dee) and zombified Jessica Holland (Christine Gordon) through the sugarcane fields to confront bug-eyed zombie Carrefore (Darby Jones); Betsy's first encounter with the somnambulistic Jessica in the haunting tower; Wesley Rand's (James Ellison) slow walk into the sea carrying the corpse of his brother's wife, the woman he loved; the drum-driven, wild dancing voodoo village sequences revealing that Mrs. Rand (Edith Barrett) is the voodoo mojo of the tribe; and the moody shipboard voyage to the West Indies where Paul Holland (Tom Conway) takes all the beautiful imagery that Betsy creates when responding to her romantic surroundings and recasts each image in decaying and vile counter-imagery. However, the movie is slow paced and the focus is too much on the half-brothers fighting over the same woman, a woman they both love, and the interference of a mother who tried to end the conflict by turning the evil Jessica into a zombie. It is almost as if Lewton instructed Tourneur to create *I Walked With a Zombie* in the image of a perverse literary Gothic classic with Byronic heroes, heavily flawed characters and an innocent nurse caught in the middle. To me the film is at its best when the visuals overpower the plot and the story is told via poetry, not melodrama. Perhaps the best section of the movie occurs when Betsy is sitting having a drink with Wesley Rand and Sir Lancelot, a Calypso singer, serenades the couple by singing a woeful ballad about the doomed Rand/Holland family. After Sir Lancelot is made aware that Rand is sitting nearby, embarrassed he humbles himself by politely apologizing for his insensitivity. When Rand responds briskly, the singer soon continues the song defiantly with complex, unspoken undercurrents. Such tension beneath the surface becomes one of the film's strengths.

And while *I Walked With a Zombie* never captivated me as it has others, it is still nevertheless a mature and brooding horror story about a drunken brother, his nihilistic half-brother and the sexily alluring nightgown-clad zombie woman Jessica, who rips the family apart. The duality of having Western educated Mrs. Rand, who runs the medical missionary to serve the natives, employ ancient voodoo practices so the tribal people will listen to her advice, becomes the major metaphor of the film. The conflict here is the duality existing between ancient tribal ways and new age medicine, just as Paul Holland's wife slowly falling in love with his half brother is a problem as old as time, but a problem treated by Mrs. Holland in cunning new ways that mesh mythos

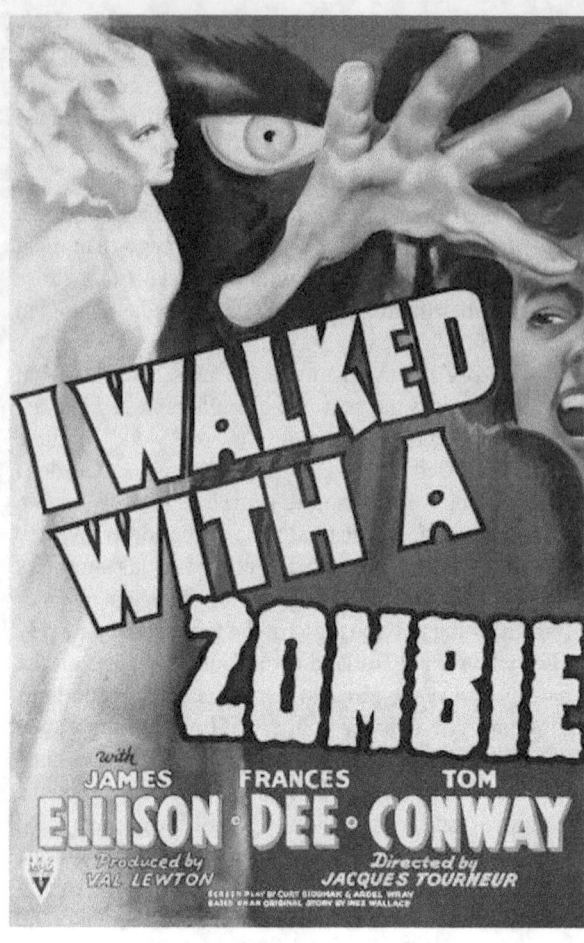

and blind faith reality. Betsy, the nurse from Canada, becomes the scientific voice of reason, who comes to believe in and accept the ways of voodoo black magic, just as Mrs. Rand has before her. Somehow the screenplay by Curt Siodmak seems to suggest that peace is restored when the new ways open up and accept the old. Close-minded devotion to rigid norms is the enemy and the innocent strength of a primitive culture offers a new way to exist in harmony with nature. The Rands-Hollands do not exist in any type of harmony, and only via the ancient ways can peace be achieved.

Perhaps Val Lewton's finest film other than *Cat People* is the totally depressing *The 7th Victim*, directed by Mark Robson. Seldom in a mainstream Hollywood movie has a film noir soaked tale of Satanism in Greenwich Village created such a morbid and absolutely hopeless vision. The film is crisp, carefully scripted and superbly directed, and the visual intensity lingers long after the final fade-out. The film pits duality against duality. We have the innocent and insular private school girl Kim Hunter voluntarily leave the womb and her security to venture to the evil city to find her missing sister, the woman who has been paying for Hunter's tuition until the payments stopped abruptly. It seems at first that elusive sister Jacqueline (Jean Brooks) may be the victim of foul play, but once the woman appears and is very much alive (her demeanor, her tentative way of acting and her distinct look burn themselves into the viewer's consciousness), we learn she is being stalked by a satanic cult operating in the big city that must kill her for revealing their private workings. In one tense sequence, all the polite occult people sit around the parlor trying to compel Jacquline to drink a class of poison wine, as they stare at her, their faces and eyes almost pleading for her to do the deed that they dare not do. Jacqueline, attracted to death and the dark side, simply refuses, flinging the glass away. In the film's best sequence, she roams the silent and haunted streets, evading one cult member with a knife, who is sent to silence her forever. Along the dark-lit and shadowy street corners, Jacquline merges with a group of theater people, who race to the nearest tavern after the performance, allowing Jacqueline a few moments of camaraderie and comfort until she is left alone at the barroom door as the fiend continues stalking her.

The film's ending is classic in its tragic implications. Elizabeth Russell, plays a young woman dying of consumption, who dreams of a life that allowing her to dress up and attend nightclubs and parties. In fact Jacqueline, her apartment neighbor, tells her to get dressed up and do the town. However, the very night the frail woman takes her advice, Jacqueline, who has a noose hanging from the ceiling of her apartment (how's that for morbidity?), commits suicide (we hear the stool turn over and then hear a thud) as the smiling Elizabeth Russell walks triumphantly past her apartment door and the end credits roll. Name a more depressing ending to a Hollywood movie.

The 7th Victim is a movie that combines so many styles and does them all well. We have the tone of film noir, as well as its shadowy look (especially those sequences filmed to approximate Greenwich Village). We have the innocent babe venturing to the evil city and, with her quest, the film becomes a mystery of what happened to my sister? The film also becomes a quasi-romantic drama when Mary (Kim Hunter) comes to be befriended by Hugh Beaumont and Erford Gage, who help her to unravel the mystery. And *The 7th Victim* even takes on the look of a crime/gangster film when the sleazy private detective takes Mary to a ware-house, walks down a lone corridor and returns moments la-ter stabbed in the gut, struggling to stay on his feet but finally dropping. In a shocking coda, when Mary is later riding a deserted train car, she sees a group of well-dressed gentle-men who are supporting the very same detective, making it appear that the dead man is merely drunk and needs some help to maneuver. Mark Robson keeps the intensity and surprises coming constantly throughout the well-stacked 71-minute film. Unlike the Universal horror chestnuts of the time, little sense of fun exists in this dark universe and the horror seems utterly real without any sense of mythos or alternative world reality.

The Body Snatcher is the favorite Val Lewton production for those people who do not take a liking to the more unconventional, eccentric and idiosyncratic Lewton productions. Don't get me wrong, *The Body Snatcher* is one of the best 1940s horror movies and contains one of Boris Karloff's finest performances, yet at the same time it seems almost a "safe" Lewton production. Although, I must admit that in tone *The Body Snatcher* continues the nihilistic thread that the finest Lewton productions contain. Director Robert Wise renders his best direction on a Lewton production and the script, co-written by Lewton himself, is focused predominantly on two characters. The actors more than rise to the occasion. Underappreciated Henry Daniell plays Dr. MacFarlane, the ice-cold scientific surgeon/teacher whose bedside manner is professional yet one that frightens crippled little girls. His adversary, the lower-class Cabman Gray (Karloff), is all smiles, kindness and warmth on the surface, yet his dark underbelly reveals pride in being able to push the renowned doctor around, literally blackmailing him because Gray saved MacFarlane from the rope when MacFarlane was a medical assistant and involved in grave-robbing discretions early on in his career. In a sense, the constant taunting and bickering that exists between the two prideful men express the film's pivotal theme that "Toddy, you'll never be rid of me!!!" In other words, the advancement of medical science is dependent upon immoral and socially unacceptable actions that must be committed. Without a steady supply of fresh corpses, medical students and veteran physicians cannot refine their craft. The snotty and arrogant doctor must kowtow to the lowly cabdriver who has knowledge that could destroy both MacFarlane's career and reputation. MacFarlane at the same time acknowledges that such nefarious activities must continue. So once again the theme of moral ambiguity comes front and center. MacFarlane hates Gray yet realizes he needs his corpses to continue being an effective surgical teacher. Gray would almost be sympathetic if it wasn't for the simple fact that he slaughters, with his shovel, the pet dog of its recently buried master. Gray transcends stealing cold-in-their-coffin corpses and starts to murder still-living victims to provide for his employment (the murder of a young, innocent and blind street singer crosses the line), making him villainous in the eyes of the audience. In his first sequence Gray is the one who gets the crippled girl to talk about her malady, while MacFarlane only frightens the child. Then in the next sequence, after Gray invites the child to pat his horse and to look for it on the street, Gray kills the pet dog and turns former audience sympathies on its ear.

The Body Snatcher is an eerie film with two spectacular sequences featuring Gray. The first pits him against the lethargic Joseph (Bela Lugosi), who attempts blackmailing the wily manipulator, but the clever cabman suffocates the easily disposed pest. The second battle is more formidable—Gray against MacFarlane, with both parties getting the better of one another until MacFarlane gets the final advantage, killing his adversary. Joseph ends up submerged in the embalming brine while Gray's corpse bounces between Fettes and MacFarlane in the carriage when MacFarlane resumes the grim duty of corpse stealing. Having stolen the recently buried corpse of a mature woman, MacFarlane is shocked to discover in each lightning bolt that her image transforms into the dead one of Gray, causing MacFarlane to crash his carriage over the side of a steep embankment. Fettes runs to his rescue only to find the doctor dead and the corpse once again that of the woman (psychologically, Gray was correct… "never be rid of me!").

The Body Snatcher is horrifying, disturbing and eerie, yet it always remains an historic drama and not a true horror movie; none of Val Lewton's productions are horror movies in the sense that Universal's *Frankenstein* and *Dracula* are. Even though the supernatural is sometimes evoked, the horrors of Lewton's universe are psychological, realistic and form the other extreme to juxtapose against Universal's mythology and fairy tale universe (just look at *Son of Frankenstein* or *The Black Cat*, let alone *Bride of Frankenstein* or *The Wolf Man*). Val Lewton productions are horror movies in the same way that Alfred Hitchcock's *Psycho* or Roger Corman's *House of Usher* are horror movies.

One of the woefully overlooked Lewton horror classics is Jacques Tourneur's *The Leopard Man*, a film so multi-layered for a seemingly simple B production that many people tend to miss its subtlety. For instance, in the film's opening sequence the tension between the two leading ladies is established within seconds. The proud and sassy Cho-Cho dances to the rat-ta-ta of her castanets, the sound of which drives American star Kiki crazy, causing the frustrated entertainer to slam her adjacent dressing room door. Prompted by her boyfriend and press agent, the beautiful Kiki enters the nightclub walking a leopard on a leash to interrupt her Mexican rival Cho-Cho, but the dancer, unfazed, snaps her castanets in rhythmic anger and frightens the cat, which escapes. This catty rivalry grows ugly when people in this quaint New Mexican town turn up dead, mauled by the apparent leopard. The cinematography of Robert de Grasse shines when the camera pans the cityscape, as Cho-Cho prances home gleefully still clicking those annoying castanets. She passes lovers kissing in the shadows, a fortune-telling card reader and says hello to friend Consuelo (Tula Parma), who is hanging out the balcony of her home. Instead of following Clo-Clo from this point, the camera now goes inside Consuela's home as she is ordered to buy corn meal for her father's supper. This leads to the pivotal sequence where the camera follows the frightened daughter as she walks across town in the dark of night, soon to be stalked by the escaped leopard who lies in wait beneath a bridge's tunnel. This terrifying Lewton walk, one of his most successful, is orchestrated by the wind and footsteps leading up to the crescendoing roar of the train suddenly passing overhead, as the leopard stares and growls. Racing back to her home, the stubbornness of a defiant mother keeps the front door closed only a few seconds too long, the screams and pool of blood flowing inside the house beneath the front door signifying the young girl's death. Such a classic sequence, and one that culminates the walk as Clo-Clo passes the cinematic baton to the youthful Consuela. Sequences such as these are ambitious and stylistic, signifying that Jacques Tourneur approached the making of *The Leopard Man* as a creative challenge and not as a quick-buck enterprise.

Another marvelous sequence occurs as a beautiful young woman carries birthday flowers to place on her father's grave in the town's cemetery. The caretaker tells the woman she is late and that the gates are locked at six. Smiling, the young girl states she will only take a moment, to which the caretaker, a crusty old man, responds, "A moment can be as just as a breath or as long as eternity." Once inside the cemetery the girl confesses at her father's grave that the flowers were only a ruse to create an excuse to meet her lover at the cemetery (which is depicted here as a gated park). However, her lover never shows and the gates are locked, and when a man offers to fetch a ladder to free her, the rustling in the tree branches signify that the leopard is near. The next morning the young girl is found dead, torn apart by the leopard, or so it seems. Now a human fiend mimics the maulings of the actual leopard (he killed the leopard and stole its teeth and claws to use as his weapons of cruelty), and *The Leopard Man* is now in Norman Bates territory with a psychopathic killer on the loose.

The Leopard Man is one of Val Lewton's finest horror offerings, but the film seldom receives kudos. The audio commentary delivered by director William Friedkin (director of The Exorcist) comes closest to crediting *The Leopard Man* for its influences on modern horror cinema. The film well deserves reappraisal for being one of the best horror films of the 1940s.

On the other side of the coin, *The Ghost Ship*, directed by Mark Robson, is the least of all the Val Lewton RKO productions and it is still a fairly decent chiller. The claustrophobic shipboard setting is low rent but Russell Wade's sympathetic third officer seaman, a victim of the crazed Captain Stone (Richard Dix), is sincere and holds audience interest. Dix's calming performance, portraying a bland but utterly believable captain, reveals the glimmer of insanity where he speaks of the captain of a ship having the power of life and death. The nuance of twisted intensity, ever so subtly revealed, makes Dix's performance better than the movie itself. After crewmen who defy the captain are accidentally killed, Russell Wade as Tom Merriam goes to

the authorities to charge the captain with the murders, but the committee laughs him off thinking such accusations an over reaction. However, Merriam finds himself returned to the captain's ship accidentally and now he is powerless to escape Stone's revenge. Even the crew believes Merriam to be a troublemaker and the men avoid him like the plague. Only mute and haunted Skelton Knaggs, in a wonderful but all too brief performance, becomes Merriam's friend and supporter and ultimately saves his life. However, The Ghost Ship is much ado about nothing and the movie seems slight and pedestrian.

Unreviewed here, *Isle of the Dead* remains one of the best Lewtons, while *Bedlam* competes on the bottom rung.

King Kong (1933)
Movie: 3.5; Disc: 4.0
Warner

King Kong is an icon production and one that influenced (and literally created) the focus on special effects in the horror, science fiction and fantasy film genre. Yes, we could go back to Willis O'Brien's *The Lost World*, but it was *King Kong* that captured the hearts and imagination of the Depression-era movie audience. For me, King Kong never quite resonated, for the film always moved at a slow pace (especially those sequences aboard the ship and when the crew first arrives on Skull Island) and the special effects stop-motion animated Kong never sparked to life with me as he did with myriad movie fans during the past 70 years. I cannot fault the production, for what it does it does well, but *King Kong* is always a movie that puts me to sleep whenever I see it, even if the presentation is at the historic Senator Theater on a giant screen with an optimal print and projection. I respect the film more than I love it.

Fay Wray becomes the iconic damsel-in-distress heroine, and her relationship with the inquisitive and playful Kong becomes the centerpiece of the movie. The other cast members are wonderful, especially Robert Armstrong's Carl Denham, whose exuberance and passion drives the film from first reel to last. The action builds slowly on the island, but Kong's confinement and escape in New York City is non-stop excitement and accounts for the film's success. *King Kong* becomes the finest example of pure action adventure in early Hollywood and well deserved the kudos.

All the revisionist theory that cast the black ape as metaphor for the enslaved black race with natives captured and taken to cruel America in chains is certainly an interesting theory, but such was never the intention of Merian C. Cooper, Ernest Schoedsak or Ruth Rose. However, such inter-pretations brought new life and interest to *King Kong* when it was rediscovered by baby boomers when it premiered on TV during the 1950s and 1960s. In fact, it was precisely during the black-is-beautiful college politics of the 1960s that *King Kong* became such a metaphor for the repression of African Americans. And when fan Wes Shank found the now deleted "censored sequences" showing Kong blatantly flatten black natives with his hefty foot and chew them alive in his mouth, the metaphor became less reasonable unless audience members claim that this was the first instance of black-on-black crime reported in cinema. Simple stated, *King Kong* is a fantasy adventure that simply entertains. However, Wes Shank's discovered footage also led to a new interpretation, with Kong's playful sniffing of Ann's undergarments and his undressing of the bound maiden. Ann Darrow (Wray) almost seems to enjoy arousing the big lug and soon writers were espousing the white woman's attraction to the powerful and larger black phallus and her rape fantasies of being powerless in the paws of the giant hairy ape. But once again, even these interpretations do not make King Kong any better or any worse.

What is most praiseworthy on this DVD remastering is the restored digital print used. Never has *King Kong* looked this good, not even in the earliest TV premiere days. One would have to go back to the theatrical reissues in the late 1930s to the early 1940s to see the movie looking this stellar, and for this reason alone *King Kong* release on DVD is a landmark one. The second disk extras include not one but two documentaries, and each is excellent in execution, although it is a sin that the man most responsible for keeping the name of *King Kong* in the modern audience's frame of reference, author Michael Price, is not interviewed or quoted or seen in any of the extras. George Turner's son Douglas is credited on screen as author of *Spawn of Skull Island,* but the truth is his contribution to that book was minimal (just compare the original *The Making of King Kong* to *Spawn of Skull Island* to realize this simple fact). Everyone seems like he is a Kong expert, but the true Kong hero, Michael Price, is nowhere to be seen or heard. This is an unforgivable oversight. But director Peter Jackson's reconstruction of the missing spider sequence, shot in black and white and aged to appear retro, is the shining moment of the DVD extras. Too bad Jackson's King Kong remake pales when compared to the reconstructed spider sequence from the original.

It is amazing that even in the era of computer-generated special effects that the creaky stop-motion animation of the Kong model creates a personality and soul that is still missing from modern CGI. King Kong is a classic film and deserves this extra special treatment, and if they survived, the Schoedsack, Cooper, O'Brien and Rose team would be standing and cheering. It does the heart good to see such a landmark movie get the treatment it so richly deserves.

Red Eye
Movie: 3.0; Disc: 3.5
DreamWorks

Wes Craven is on a roll, and unlike most of his contemporaries from the 1970s, Craven is still working steadily and appears to be at the top of his game. George Romero faltered in the 1990s and only recently returned with two new zombie entries. John Carpenter still works occasionally, but his most recent movies such as *Vampires* and *Ghosts of Mars* are lesser works when compared to *Halloween* and *The Thing*. Craven, unlike many of his peers, has been able to evolve from B horror to mainstream drama (*Music of the Heart*) and mainstream horror (the *Scream* trilogy). Even his other film released a few years ago, *Cursed*, is a terrific horror offering that recalls all of Craven's strengths as a master craftsman.

Red Eye is a thriller, one cut in the Alfred Hitchcock or Brian De Palma mold, yet Craven uses all his horror film tricks to breathe life and vitality into the suspense (sudden shocks, pens thrust into Adam's apples, claustrophobic horror in airplane restrooms, the fiend chasing a vulnerable female through her home, fear caused by thunderstorms, etc.). Gratefully confined to an hour and 25 minutes, *Red Eye* gets to the point and does not wear its welcome out. The cast is focused primarily on two people, our heroine Rachel McAdams (Lisa) and our political assassin Cillian Murphy (Jackson Rippner). After being introduced in a flirtatious manner, Lisa and Jackson find themselves sharing two adjacent seats on the airplane to Florida. Within a few minutes of friendly banter, Jackson reveals that he is in fact an assassin and, unless Lisa does as she is told, a hit man outside her father's home will kill him within minutes of receiving a phone call. The manner in which the tone of the conversation is revealed, he at first casually making light of his career, then dropping the bombshell, only demonstrates what a fine reactive actress McAdams is. Lisa's eyes fill with tears that bathe her cheeks as her expression goes blank and her universe crashes within a matter of seconds. Jackson punctuates the conversation with a quickly delivered head butt that renders the young woman unconscious, and Jackson carefully plops her head on the airplane pillow making it seem the woman is napping. Jackson has to wipe his bleeding forehead only moments before the flight attendance stops by to ask if everything's all right. For this entire middle act of the movie, the action is primarily focused, in tight cuts, on the duo speaking dialogue that somehow manages to mesmerize and hold its audience's attention. On one hand Lisa is slow to submit to Jackson's demands, and when she is told to call her hotel (she is a upper-level manager and can arrange for dignitaries to have their rooms changed) to switch the suite of a homeland security official to another suite, she wants guarantees that first her father is still alive and that Jackson will phone his assassin accomplice as soon as she makes the phone call. And when the crafty woman agrees to make the call, the raging thunderstorm knocks out all phone connections, so the suspense heightens. During the coming minutes Lisa will attempt to write a warning note in a paperback book she loans one of the passengers, and will write a message in soap on the restroom mirror. However Jackson enters the restroom as soon as she exits and sees the message before anyone else does. Then under the pretense of having a "quickie" in the bathroom, Jackson is able to terrify his victim even more—within very close quarters. This airplane sequence is punctuated with a tremendous sequence. That's when Lisa plunges her hidden ballpoint pen into his Adam's apple, rendering the man speechless so he cannot make his phone call, as she rushes to exit the plane before he can recover his faculties.

From this point onward the final third of the film involves chases through malls, cars darting across town and two professional assassins pursuing Lisa in her own home after her father has been rendered unconscious by the first hit man. Lisa bears a knife scar on her chest above her breast, the result of a daylight rape a few years earlier, and she swears that she won't be the victim ever again. Rachel McAdam's performance is one of empowerment, whether it is in her capacity as manager at work or as wily victim aboard the plane. The slam-bang manner in which she is finally able to phone her hotel and have the homeland security official and her family moved, just before terrorists launch an anti-tank missile directly into the hotel suite, is cinematic nail-biting intensity at its best.

Red Eye is a powerful popcorn movie and nothing more, but with an intelligent script, superb direction and wonderful acting it seems richer and more profound.

Hostel
Movie: 3.0; Disc: 3.5
Sony/TriStar

Eli Roth's debuting feature was the impressive *Cabin Fever*, a horror programmer inspired by the horror films of the 1970s, with a firm foot in the future, playfully creating a tone that veers from intense horror to almost comical splatter. *Cabin Fever* promised a great future for the talented writer/director.

Hostel, in many ways, lives up to the reputation of *Cabin Fever* and then some. However, the sequences depicting intense physical torture do tend to go over the top and become rather disturbing. After establishing good guy Josh (Derek Richardson) as the responsible one (his equally stoned friends pay for a prostitute to help him get over an emotionally draining breakup, but he runs out the door about the time the hottie takes off her bra), the sequence that shows him striped to his underpants, shackled to a chair and having a demented Dutch Businessman literally dissect him is not entertainment to me. It is unclear if Roth wanted his audience to cower and grimace and look away or hoot and holler and cheer the torturer on. Along with the Saw franchise, we see the birth of torture porn. Sick is sick. At least horny and stoned Icelander Oli (Evthor Gudjonsson) quietly disappears, but he sends his friends a cell phone photo with the text message that he went home. The audience next sees the phone photo is actually a

shot of the dismembered head of Oli sitting on a table, giving the viewers their first glimpse that this is not *National Lampoon's East European Vacation*. So when survivor Paxton (Jay Hermandez) is tortured by a German surgeon (Patr Janis), viewers think he is headed down the same highway to hell as buddy Josh. When the chainsaw wielding surgeon slips on Paxton's blood and severs his own leg, this gives Josh the chance to grab a pistol, pick up his two severed fingers and have a chance to escape with his life. Don't get me wrong, *Hostel* is intense and directed creatively with superb East European locations and dank sets, photographed majestically. I just question the subject matter and the degree to which torture is depicted. However, I do admit the film's imagery has become cemented in my imagination, a credit to the filmmakers.

What I find most commendable here are the characters created by Hernandez and Richardson, horny stoners out for a hedonistic backpack tour of Europe. In one sense these horny bastards deserve everything they get, but in this case their punishment does not fit their crimes. The bevy of Eastern European beauties that populate the film are hot and Roth likes to show them in various stages of nudity. The girls, who populate a hostel, work in teams and always operate with the same pattern. When the newly registered guys learn they have to share a room with the ladies, the ladies are always half dressed when the guys enter, but the girls are flirtatious and invite the guys to join them in the spa. The women are paid handsomely to recruit both males and females to be human fodder for an exclusive "club" whose members pay thousands of dollars to rent private dungeons with human victims, where they can torture and kill them in any way that turns them on. In the best performance of the film, Paxton escapes when he comes upon a man who is about to enter his personal dungeon, and the man asks Paxton how it was (thinking Paxton was the person who paid, not the unfortunate victim who should be dismembered) and whether he should finish the person off rapidly or take his time. The man's enthusiasm and perversity shines as one of the best performances in the film. The character of the Dutch businessman, past middle age and balding, who rides the trains and chats strangers about his beautiful daughter and his wonderful life, all the while eating salad with his fingers, is rather odd and perverse. When it turns out he is the torturer of Josh, everything is put into its proper perspective. And of course after Paxton's escape from the funhouse from hell, he happens to come upon this same man in a restroom, where he carries out his own revenge for a departed friend, the Dutchman having his own fingers severed and throat slit, choking with his head pushed down in the toilet.

Eli Roth's script works because of the close attention to details. The script has Paxton suffering guilt over allowing a child to drown that he might have saved, and when he escapes from the torture dungeon, a female's screams create the chance for redemption that eluded him years ago as he reenters the dungeon to save the woman, an Asian girl he briefly met at the hostel, whose half face has been gored and burned and her one eye ball dangles down the side of her cheek… blood everywhere. Also the introduction of the terrifying bubble-gum gang of children and their final attack upon the torturers' car, heavy rocks fall from above smashing the villains' heads, is oddly satisfying. Such touches linger in the mind, especially the totally enraptured couple, totally naked, making love on the sofa, while Oli takes a chair and stares and his two buddies make friends with the naked man's roommate who tells him where to find the hottest girls in Slovakia (he too works with the prostitutes to lure unsuspecting victims to the torture dungeon). While it might be easy to dismiss *Hostel* as a glorified "snuff" movie, the film's artistry and intelligence make it something superior.

Hostel bears close parallels with Sean Cunningham's *Last House on the Left*, with its intensity of torture, murder and revenge, and the Dutch Businessman reminds me more than a little of the similar character in the original version of *The Vanishing*. But beyond this, *Hostel* is totally original. The film's visuals linger for a long, long time. Extras include audio commentaries and an extended documentary.

Dreams in the Witch House
[*Masters of Horror* Showtime]
Movie: 2.0; Disc: 3.5
Anchor Bay

For those of us who did not subscribe to Showtime's anthology series *Masters of Horror*, Anchor Bay released the series to DVD, this first entry co-written and directed by Stuart Gordon, based upon the classic short story by H.P. Lovecraft. While this anthology series only permits 55 minute movies on a limited budget, the Showtime connection does allow hard R nudity and violence and it is once again intriguing to see the 2006-2007 take on horror via the anthology TV series.

Dreams in the Witch House covers all the iconic Gordon bases—college graduate student (who wears the Miskatonic University tee shirt) as both hero and victim, a reading of the dreaded Necronomicon, dimensional crossovers, demonic possession and a good guy who commits horrible acts. Youthful Ezra Godden (Walter) is this generation's Jeffrey Combs and beautiful yet hardened Chelah Horsdal becomes the new Barbara Crampton. Once again Stuart Gordon's cinematic Lovecraftian world is different from the literary one, but the telemovie's mood and sense of horror excels. After Walter rents a room in a 300-year-old apartment building so he can pursue his grad degree, he meets neighbor Frankie (Francis), who is a single mom, out of work, with an infant baby. The two strike it right off and Walter has to loan Frankie some money so

she is not evicted by tubby, tee shirt-stained landlord Mr. Dombrowski (Jay Brazeau). In the meanwhile Walter has violent nightmares, dreaming that a rat with a human face comes to speak to him during the night. His nightmares also feature the vision of a witch, as though demonic forces from another dimension merge with our own. One evening Frankie asks Walter to babysit while she goes to an interview, and when she returns she finds Walter locked outside her apartment banging on the door to get back inside, the baby unattended. Walter admits he fell asleep, but now he fears he sleepwalks, and he does not wish to blow his budding relationship. That night in his dreams the vision of the witch appears, seductive, undressing, now totally naked, and, emerging from the shadows, the face of the witch is now Frankie's. As the two embrace and lock lips, the witch's fingernails scratch Walter's back into a bloody pulp, but as they physically interlock, Frankie's face fades and the festered and aged body of a cackling white-haired crone replaces the sensual youthful body of Frankie.

The plot grows more horrifying as the witch demands a blood sacrifice, the murder of Frankie's baby. While in his dreams, Walter fights to protect and save the child's life, but the demonic human-faced rat ultimately rips into the infant's neck, killing the infant, the dead child cuddled in Walter's arms as the mother comes upon the scene. Walter is soon committed to an asylum where he rants about his dreams of the witch and rat and maintains his own innocence, while another elderly tenant in the apartment house, a weird old man who encountered the same dreams as Walter, punishes himself for his own crimes by ritualistically bashing his head against a bureau top to atone for his sins. Of course no happy ending exists in Stuart Gordon's evil world.

Dreams in the Witch House is wonderful hour-long television, but the quality is not worthy of theatrical release. As one episode of a Showtime anthology series, it satisfies, but it has all been done before and done better and it seems more like the best of Stuart Gordon retread rather than something innovative and new. Again the two leads do wonderful work and the cinematography and direction produce a creepy mood. However the blue-tinged cinematography whenever Walter dreams becomes gimmicky in a corny manner. The best sequences of *Dreams in the Witch House* suggest superior Stuart Gordon projects, but for Showtime the series is most intriguing.

Perhaps the disk's best aspects are its supplementals, and they are plentiful. We have audio commentary tracks, a making of documentary, interviews with Stuart Gordon about making the film, an interview with Chelah Horsdal, a special effects documentary, still/storyboard gallery and a DVD-ROM reprinting of the original Lovecraft story.

Cigarette Burns [*Masters of Horror* Showtime]
Movie: 3.0; Disc: 3.5
Anchor Bay

Cigarette Burns, the 59-minute short feature directed by John Carpenter from the Showtime series *Masters of Horrors*, improves upon the episode directed by Stuart Gordon. On the other hand, *Cigarette Burns* is positively weird and unnerving and seems unlike any other John Carpenter film yet produced. And this is exactly what the *Masters of Horror* series should provide for these veterans of horror cinema... a forum for them to be creative, experimental and attempt to recreate and refocus their cinematic vision. And Carpenter more than rises to the occasion, producing an hour-long scarefest that grows weirder by every minute. The film's vision is very European and Carpenter appears to be more than a tad influenced by the similar work of Lamberto Bava and Dario Argento (whose name is referred to reverentially in the film). And while a few sequences seem out of place or simply over the top, most of the 59-minute production works to get under the skin.

John Carpenter was a fan (who produced a fanzine and made super 8mm home monster movies) before he went professional, and *Cigarette Burns* thrives on its film-geek adrenalin rush. First of all, the plot involves the obsessive nature of collectors and explores the lengths a person will go to add a rare item to the collection. The fact that the object of obsession is a one-of-a-kind surviving 35mm movie print (of a cult film called *La Fin Absolue du Monde*) only adds more appeal to Carpenter's niche audience. In other words this is a horror movie made for horror movie fans, and while mainstream releases may not be able to cater to a specialized audience, the *Masters of Horror* episode certainly can.

The acting for the most part is excellent, and Euro-cult star Udo Keir (Mr. Ballinger) does himself proud as the rich and obsessive film collector who dreams every night of owning a copy of *La Fin Absolue du Monde*. Ex-drug addict Kirby (Norman Reedus), the owner/operator of a small revival horror movie theater, is in debt to his father-in-law for $200,000. It seems after loaning Kirby the money, the father-in-law's daughter, heavily strung-out, slices her wrists in the bathtub and dies. Her death haunts Kirby but his father-in-law's mob-style demands for immediate payback forces him to accept the task of finding a print of the movie for Ballinger, and the mystery begins. Kirby's journey takes him to a reclusive movie critic who is all but retired and writing the definitive review of *La Fin Absolue du Monde*, the piles of neatly staked typed paper occupying his entire abode. Soon Kirby encounters a weird, gonzo/extreme filmmaker

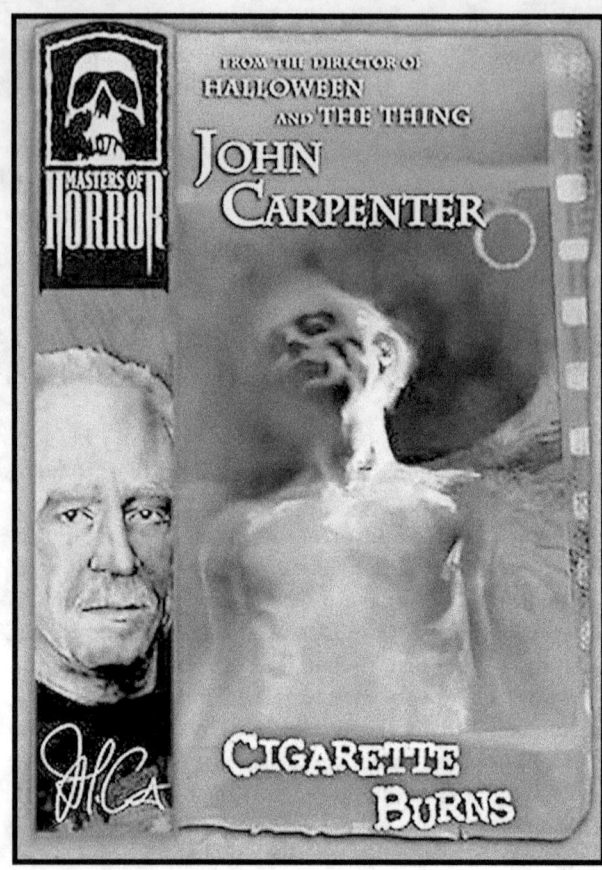

who forces Kirby to watch as he beheads a young woman on screen with a machete. The sequence is the one that hits a false note and seems only to exist to showcase the splatter effects by Greg Nicotero and Howard Berger. The sequence following the beheading where the bald, leather-garbed director sits on the bound lap of Kirby and gets right in his face by sharing his nightmares is truly creepy, but the special effects sequence is really not necessary.

Once the lost film is recovered and Ballinger screens the movie, watching it with his servant Fung (Colin Foo), things get really weird. The short clips we get to see of the movie, black and white, are never as innovative as the short video from *The Ring* for instance, but the standard horror sequences depicted (a broken fingernail scraping against a stone wall) do make the viewer desire to see more. After the screening Ballinger cuts out his intestines and runs them through his projector, while Fung, his entire torso covered with knife wounds, takes a dagger to both eyes and cuts them out. When Kirby arrives he too watches part of the movie and sees the haunting nude figure of his dead girl friend, covered in blood, reminding him of the horrors of his past life, and in desperation Kirby takes a pistol to his mouth and blows his brains out. It seems people who watch *La Fin Absolue du Monde* are haunted by their past digressions and personal failings. For each individual the film creates a vision of their personal hell, causing them to commit violent acts of mayhem and self-destruction.

Yes, yes, yes, specific sequences could have been better executed and some of the self-indulgence would be better off truncated. However, within *Cigarette Burns* is a classic horror movie crying to come out, a movie that challenges John Carpenter's viewers unlike any of his movies made within the last 20 years. Again, we may even consider the film to be a failure, but it's a damn interesting one and its sense of foreboding mystery simply captivates the viewer. Many sequences are spectacular and the innovative ideas here overrule the banal. For the first time in ages John Carpenter is stretching and trying to find his creative soul once again. Strangely, Carpenter did not compose the musical score himself as usual, but the typical Carpenter-sounding music was composed by one Cody Carpenter, perhaps the director's son?

Supplementals abound and include audio commentaries, four documentaries, a Carpenter bio and still gallery. Anchor Bay really pulled out all the stops for their releases of the *Masters of Horror* series.

Incident On and Off a Mountain Road
[*Masters of Horror* Showtime]
Movie: 3.5; Disc: 3.5
Anchor Bay

So far the *Masters of Horror* Showtime series have been hit and miss. The Stuart Gordon was mediocre while the John Carpenter entry was original and bold. However, Don Cos-carelli's Incident *On and Off a Mountain Road* is simply an exceptional hour chiller, directed by the man who brought us *Phantasm* and *Bubba Ho-Tep*. This story uses the hour running time to perfection, creating a multi-layered story of subtlety and finesse that would have seemed padded if the story were expanded to 90 minutes.

I love movies that are book-ended; that is, they begin and end on the same unsettling image, in this case a close-up of a woman's partial face and eye. The story is two-fold. Its back-story tells of a young woman Ellen (Bree Turner) who meets and falls in love with a wacko survivalist Bruce (Ethan Embry), a very intense young man. As the horror drama unfolds, we intersperse the current sequences of horror with Bruce and Ellen's relationship building and ultimately melting as Bruce turns more and more abusive, forcing Ellen to come at him with a knife.

In the current story an intense Ellen is driving alone at night on the mountain road where she suddenly comes upon an abandoned car in the middle of the road that she rear-ends. Inside the abandoned car Ellen finds blood stains and she goes off to explore. Looking over the embankment she sees a strange figure wearing a floppy hat start to stagger up the hill, but as the figure approaches, Ellen sees he is dragging a struggling woman who screams for help. Taking off his hat, the demonic fiend known as Moonface appears, a classically haunting monster played to perfection by John De Santis. Ellen is first seen as the weak and frightened female victim, but soon her survivalist training comes into play when she literally leaps over the embankment and rolls down the hill, setting booby traps for Moonface and cleverly outwitting the equally clever fiend. However, the female mistakenly runs toward one of Ellen's traps and the poor woman gets her leg impaled on a sharp wooden stake. In this clever about-face, Ellen becomes the heroic predator who refuses to die. Even when she is captured and locked in Moonface's rural cabin basement, she uses her skills to escape.

Moonface is akin to the Ray Milland character in *X, The Man With X Ray Eyes*, in that both believe if thy eye offends thee... cut it out. Moonface believes that seeing evil becomes evil, so he has a huge drill in the basement that he uses to drill out the eyes (clean through the entire skull!) of his victims, and then he hangs the bodies, scarecrow style, on poles in his field. Perennial Coscarelli superstar Angus Scrimm appears in a cameo role as Buddy, a crazy old man who appears to be a victim of Moonface, but he is actually more a partner in crime. Everything Buddy states is hyperbole with wide eyes

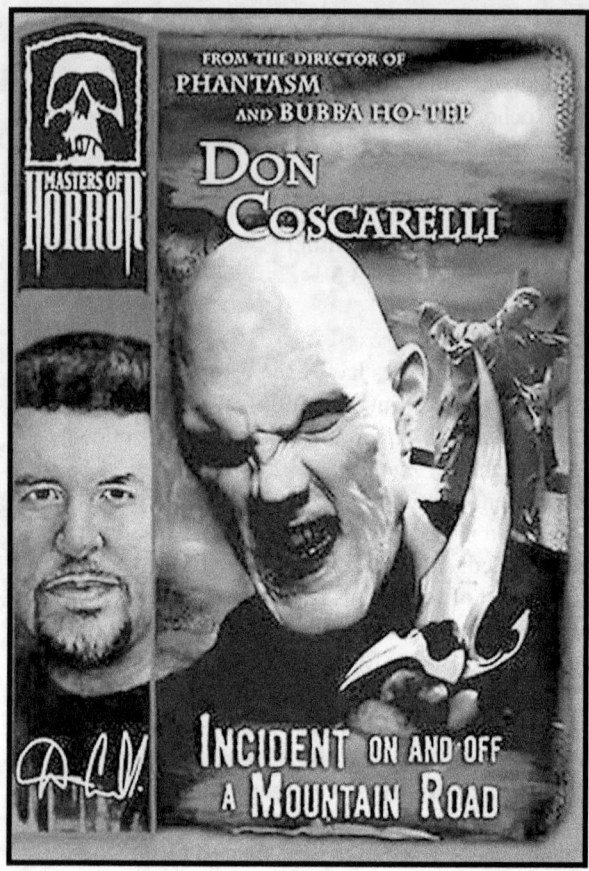

and a folksy calm delivery. He is a wonderfully quirky character and Scrimm does a stellar job of bringing the lunatic to life. However, the audience feels relieved when Ellen savagely puts the old fool out of his misery.

By the show's end everyone is dead except for Ellen, and guess who she has hidden in the trunk of her car? Yes, her abusive husband is dead, and cleverly, she carries him to Moonface's drill and takes out both eyes and mounts him out in the field... just another innocent victim of the horrifying fiend. The hour ends as Ellen returns to her car and, just as intensely as when she arrived, leaves, the camera again closing in on her eye and face.

Incident On and Off a Mountain Road is utter perfection. The acting of Turner, Scrimm and De Santis all congeal to produce a symphony of horror, a nightmare of ultra-violence that does not push the buttons to the same extent as the recent *The Devil's Rejects, Hostel* or *Wolf Creek*, thank God! Instead the cinematography and editing produce a nightmare chase with strong character development. The manner in which both stories are merged is always cinematic and a credit to director Coscarelli. Magnificent shots of the pitch-black night framed by the gigantic full moon and Moonface's slow motion jump in front of that moon is the archetype of classic horror. Even though the character of Moonface is cast from the same mold as Freddy or Jason, for some strange reason this film seems less exploitative and more in the traditional horror film mold. One thing is certain; the tone is horrific without the embarrassing inclusion of wink-wink-nudge-nudge humor. Moonface is a classic horror fiend for the ages.

Anchor Bay is to be commended for the wonderful supplementals included on this DVD, including interviews and audio commentary with Don Cascarelli, several making-of documentaries, still and trailer gallery, a Cascarelli biography, etc. The mythology of horror has been ignored as of late, but *An Incident On and Off a Mountain Road* reminds us why mythology and horror go hand in hand.

Sick Girl [*Masters of Horror* Showtime]
Movie: 3.0; Disc: 3.5
Anchor Bay

At first I said, who the hell is Lucky McKee and how did he get to be a *Master of Horror* so rapidly? Simply stated, Roger Corman dropped out of the series at the last moment and McKee, director of the highly rated indie horror movie *May*, got the nod to join the elite ranks (McKee is the youngest *Master of Horror* in the series).

Surprisingly, *Sick Girl* is an absolute delight, a quirky and almost poignant lesbian love affair that slowly and creepily evolves into full-blown horror along the lines of *The Wasp Woman* or *The Fly*. The two female stars are absolutely perfect, with Angela Bettis playing the eccentric entomologist (bug scientist in other words) who turns her apartment into a bug zoo, frequently with beautiful insects wondering free. This scientist Ida is the bane of her landlord, a crusty old woman who does not wish any complaints from the other tenants and the thought of an apartment of bugs freaks her out. The lonely scientist is attracted to an odd hippie-style free-spirited girl who sits in the apartment lobby sketching fairies. Soon Ida builds up the courage to ask the beautiful young girl (Erin Brown aka Misty Mundae) to dinner and the two hit it off. During their first date at Ida's apartment, all the bugs are moved to the bedroom, allowing the innocent couple to connect. When Ida asks Misty if she needs some pajamas and privacy after downing too much hard liquor, the enchanting vixen peals off her top, exposing herself, and coyly purrs, she doesn't need any privacy. The almost PG lesbian make-out scene follows and true love flourishes.

However, about the same time Ida receives a mysterious box containing an unknown species of insect that soon breaks loose in Ida's apartment and makes a nest in a pillow on her bed. When Misty rests there, the insect infects her ear and soon begins swapping bodily juices. This of course leads to a change in personality for Misty and ultimately her mutation into a semi-insect-human with bugged-out eyes with tentacles erupting from her body. Ultimately both girls are infected and both become pregnant, a clever trick of Misty's professor father who realizes that pregnant lesbians are few and far between.

Sick Girl shines by virtue of its warm and cuddly characterizations created by Bettis and Brown. Both quirky and shy, the audience wants these eccentric girls to get together as they seemingly make the perfect match for one another. Especially after Misty announces her father is an entomologist and that she was raised around weird bugs and loves them as well. Sick Girl develops mostly as a chick flick romantic relationship movie, and the horror enters a little at a time. The first sign of the terror aspect is when Misty pulls back the hair over her ear and feels a slimy pus. Soon Misty develops a more assertive personality and a profane mouth. And finally she develops a more aggressive sexuality that belies her former conservative personality. The spunky little insect, a mechanical live-action critter, is both fascinating and horrific, and when its pinchers penetrate human flesh and impregnate its human victims, the episode becomes downright kinky. The climax occurs when Misty becomes the bug-human mutant causing the unfortunate landlady to do a belly-flop over the second story banister. The mutant then sucks the life out of Ida's male friend, who is left a bloody pulp of human debris.

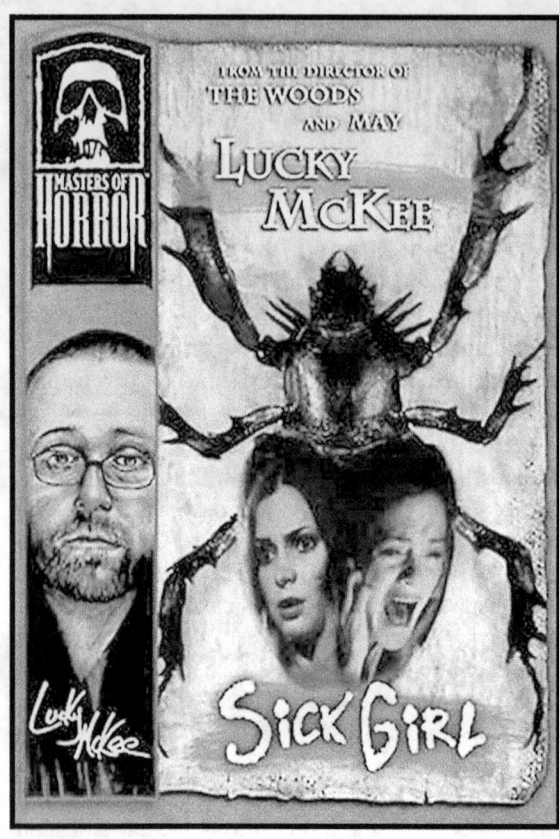

Odd, charming, sexy, romantic and ultra-violent are all adjectives that describe *Sick Girl* to perfection. The direction by Lucky McKee is sure-handed and he does an amazing job creating a vacillating tone that veers seamlessly from the romantic to the horrific. His performances all resonate and become realistic in the most quirky of ways. Overall, *Sick Girl* is the most odd and truly original entry in the *Masters of Horror* series so far. As usual the bios, interviews with cast and crew and making-of documentary are excellent. And it goes to show one hour running times can often be enough.

The Exorcism of Emily Rose
Movie: 3.0; Disc: 3.5
Sony

Critics were tepid when it came to *The Exorcism of Emily Rose*, but to me, the movie was above average, terrifying and thought provoking. Imagine a courtroom drama horror thriller. That more upscale approach allowed Laura Linney and Tom Wilkerson to take the lead roles of defense attorney and haunted priest. Even unknown Jennifer Carpenter as Emily Rose does stellar work, both as the possessed demon teenager and as the prim and proper college student.

Scott Derrickson directs and co-writes, and his drama of moral dilemma is stronger than the horror presentation, I must be honest. From the horror aspect, the movie shines best when Carpenter distorts her body and strikes a pose, literally frozen in time. The cheap shocks are always punctuated by bombastic musical cues written by Christopher Young. His musical score is quite effective if sometimes guilty of overkill. However, in the first sequence where Emily is possessed, when even the nighttime storm clouds reflect a demonic visage, the visual horror is very nicely executed. After the poor student is possessed, she rushes down the college campus walkway at night and every face suddenly morphs into a howling contortion of evil. The exorcism sequences themselves are dramatic and off-putting, but nothing here can rival similar sequences from The Exorcist, the film that did it first and best (not the movie, but the exorcism sequences specifically). Creepy and easily getting uncomfortable under the skin, the cinematography maintains tension and interest.

However, the drama shines brightest in its courtroom sequences where the priest accused of murder only wishes to tell Emily's story on the stand, but the church diocese wants to muzzle the priest from embarrassing the church and several times throughout the movie Laura Linney's character is reminded that she is being paid by the church and that she works for their best interests. The script plays very fair and presents both the moral and psychological side of the drama, with Wilkerson's low-key performance as the priest both realistic and sympathetic. The script tilts the balance at times in favor of the priest's views and at other times in favor of the mainstream establishment who claims that Emily Rose suffered from a form of psycho-epilepsy that made her unbalanced. It is at the priest's insistence that she abandons medically prescribed drugs, this being the direct cause of her death. The movie does not wish to take sides but to offer a rationale for both points of view, allowing the audience to decide what is the right and wrong here. And the ambiguity of the plot only complicates matters and makes a clear-cut answer impossible to obtain. Even the movie's ending, with the jury delivering a guilty verdict, but then suggesting a sentencing that all but eliminates the guilty verdict, seems like a cop-out that allows all sides to win. It might be clever filmmaking that nobody loses, but the ending lessens the power of the actual trial and the arguments made within.

The DVD extras are a nice mix of multiple documentaries, director audio commentary and deleted scenes.

When a Stranger Calls
Movie: 2.5; Disc: 3.0
Columbia

Horror movies were not at their creative peak in 1979, and *When a Stranger Calls*, better than most, only illustrates how effective movies such as *Halloween* actually were. Instead of Jamie Leigh Curtis as the babysitter, we have innocent and youthful Carol Kane as the high schooler, armed with school books, who is all set to hunker down and study, while a doctor and his wife go out to dinner and a movie. Luckily the kids are already up in bed asleep and the parents tell the babysitter Jill to not disturb them. *When a Stranger Calls* is at its intense best during the film's first 15 minutes and its final 15... in between is simply psycho-babble and filler. This film would have made a wonderful half hour TV horror anthology, but stretched out to 97 minutes, it's a frizzle. The personable Jill starts to received phone calls from a husky-voiced male who asks, "Have you checked the children lately?" Of course the intelligent teen rightfully ignores such prank calls, but soon she phones the police and they act as though she is creating the prank. The horror gets intense when the police finally (and reluctantly) trace the phone call and discover it originates inside the house where Jill is phoning. The police order her to leave the house immediately, but before she does, shadows and noises from upstairs frighten both her and the audience, especially when she goes up the second floor steps and hears a noise coming from one of the upper rooms. In a panic she runs down and scrambles to unlock the front door, when she runs head long into the stoic and massive body of police detective Charles Durning, in one of his first noticeable film roles. Unfortunately we learn that the psycho killer is phoning from the children's bedroom where he has slaughtered them savagely. This sequence works

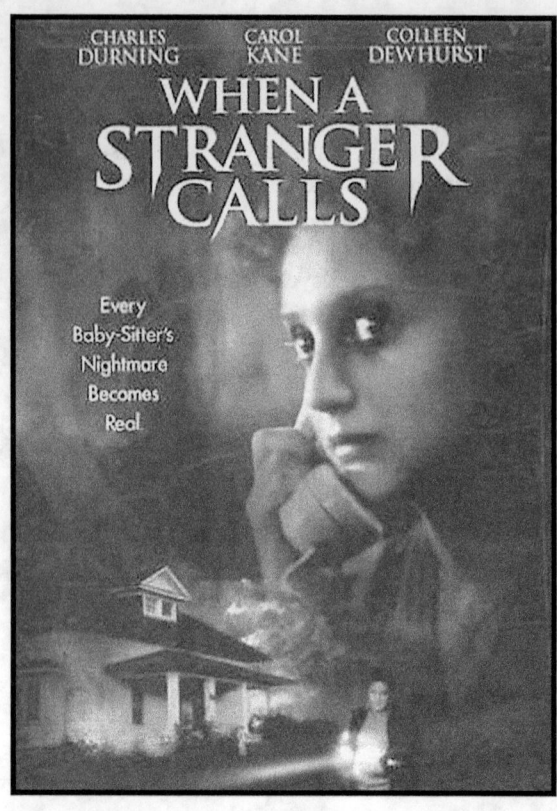

as an extended variation of what the first Scream movie did with the Drew Barrymore character. The direction by writer-director Fred Walton is nearly perfect, and Carol Kane's frightened innocent is a powerful if stereotyped performance.

To dovetail this fine beginning, the movie picks up seven years later with Jill now married with two children of her own, children just about the same age as the children slaughtered in the film's opening sequence. In a parallel ending, Jill and her husband are doing the town while another dedicated babysitter watches their children... when Jill gets a phone call at the restaurant asking, "Have you checked the children lately?" Of course our psycho has escaped from the asylum and Charles Durning, now a private detective, is hired to bring the loon back to his padded cell. Back at the restaurant, Jill collapses, screams and cries and has her husband race home. Arriving home, he finds the babysitter relaxed and calm and the children nestled calmly in bed. Of course after the audience breathes a collective sigh of relief, we find that the fiend is already inside the house and eliminates the husband before coming after Jill and the children. Before the final curtain Charles Durning makes another appearance and the movie ends as a non-stop roller coaster ride that once again satisfies. Again, the middle third (actually half) is pedestrian and lags, but what this movie is really about is the initial sequence and its parallel closing one.

Even though the DVD box claims the movie has been remastered in high definition, the print used is typically smeary with non-descript color, as were most horror movies of that era. *When a Stranger Calls* is mediocre with a few intense sequences that rise it above the typical horror chiller of its era.

Wolf Creek
Movie: 3.0; Disc: 3.5
Dimension

Horror movies of the new millennium are worshipping at the altar of 1970s horror, with their inflated budgets trying to improve upon lower-budgeted independent productions created 30 years earlier. *Wolf Creek* is an Australian low-budgeter that attempts to create an Aussie Freddy Krueger or Jason Voorhees. Instead we get a cross between Crocodile Dundee and the late Sam Irwin. The movie is well done and nicely acted, and the moody Outback bush photography is quite breathtaking and literally becomes a major character in the movie. However, the basic story is one we have seen a few too many times and the twists are now clichés. Director Greg McLean does have a nice style and, with more original material, he may some day produce a classic horror movie, but this is not it.

Once again, just like the similar *Hostel*, the leading characters are introduced as non-stop partying young adults, who strike the audience as being more pathetic than sympathetic. So it takes a while for the trio to develop their multi-layered human persona that allows the audience to care for them. Even then, we barely do so when these two women and one man are terrified and tortured, the dramatic impact is not as great as it could have been. Out in the Aussie boondocks with a dead car, the too chatty but very warm Mick Taylor (John Jarratt) wins over the frightened young adults who think him the bees knees for taking his time to tow them back to his settlement, a deserted mining camp. There he methodically inspects and works on their car while providing them shelter and food. In his opening monologue, Jarratt manages to be warm in telling funny little anecdotes, until he begins to focus on his job, that of hunting down animals from a helicopter and killing pigs with his knife. Ben (Nathan Phillips) then remarks how lucky Mick must be, having his freedom to roam nature, but Mick's smiling face, not quite figuring out whether this young man is praising him (which he is doing) or making fun of him (which Mick's expression seems to imply), listens until he is asked what he does now. Mick, returning to the center focus with his overdone smile, states he could tell them, but then he would have to kill them, before erupting into a demented giggle that foreshadows the horrors to come. But Jarratt's performance is both bravado and subtlety combined and he produces a very unsettling villain. As the two girls settle down around the camp fire and fall asleep, the HD video camera fades to black for several seconds before returning to focus on one of the girls, Liz (Cassandra Magrath), now tied up and alone in a small storage room, signifying the polite introductions are over and the horror is beginning. The second girl, Kristie (Kestie Morassi), tied to a wooden pole, screaming hysterically, half-dressed and bloodied, is terrified when Mick threatens to shoot her with a hunting rifle, but when he tires of terrifying her, he rubs his crotch and begins to molest her, holding a knife to her throat, as Liz gets the drop on Mick and shoots him in the neck. Of course Mick survives. Poor Ben awakens to find himself nailed to a wooden crucifix where he has to literally find the strength to pull his arms from the spikes to free himself.

Wolf Creek develops in predictable ways as the girls split up, Liz venturing out alone to try to find a vehicle (Mick collects all the cars of all the victims he kills) while Kristie hides in the bush. However, in a sequence similar to the money shot from *House of 10,000 Corpses* (another homage to 1970s horror cinema), Kristie is rescued by an elderly man, who stops alongside the road to offer her help, but a sudden shot from Mick's rifle blows his eye and the back of his head off while Kristie, almost in shock, crawls away on her hands and knees, Mick waits and waits until the right time occurs for him to deliver the death blow, in a quiet sequence punctuated by the single rifle blast. The sequence is wonderfully directed and photographed. Liz meets the

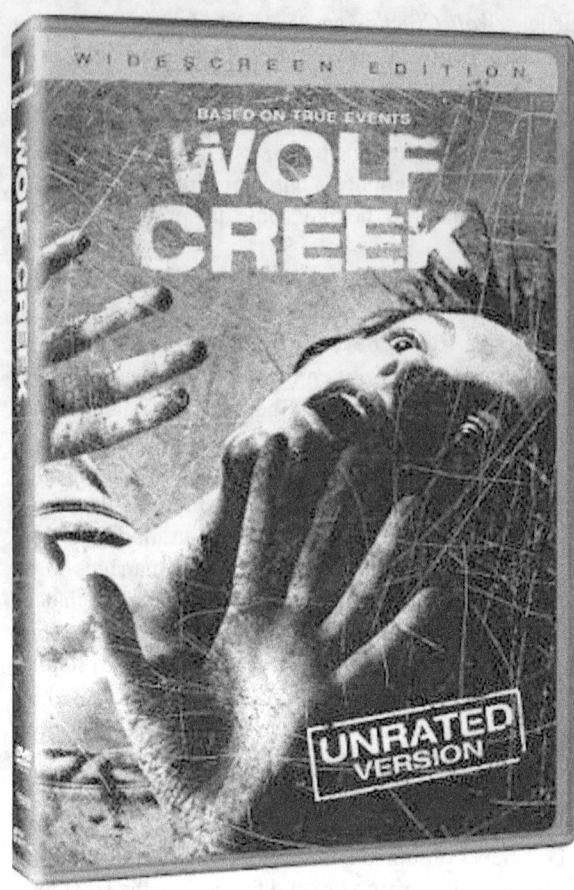

hunter's blade as Mick drives the knife into her back, severing her spinal cord, as she drops to the dirt, her eyes opened wide in pain, shock and death. But such sequences of intense and unrelenting horror is what Wolf Creek is all about. Just like *Hostel*, it's all about torture and slow ritualistic death, served straight up. The film is what it is, and while it is done well, it is not particularly original or pleasant. The young victims are more than competent and John Jarratt's performance does steal the show.

Extras include an audio commentary, a deleted sequence and a mesmerizing making of documentary that demonstrates the wonderful textures that HD video can capture (the video was transferred to 35mm). And the interviews with Jarratt and how he prepared for his fiendish role are quite entertaining. To me such torture-horror nightmares are not my idea of entertainment, but I must admit that *Wolf Creek* had me spellbound, more so by the haunting visuals than by the gruesome murders.

Room 6
Movie: 3.0; Disc: 3.5
Anchor Bay

Variations on classics such as Carnivals of Souls are usually interesting, as the Herk Harvey cult classic does offer an innovative take on the ghost movie. *Room 6*, co-written and directed by Mike Hurst, is a movie that seems influenced by the spirit of *Carnival of Souls*. In the earlier film, a beautiful young woman is involved in an automobile crash on a bridge, and she thinks she is miraculously saved and goes on with her life, being visited by ghastly apparitions from the dead that ultimately claim her. Finally, the audience learns that she never survived the incident on the bridge. In *Room 6* we have another car crash victim, but one who does not immediately die. Instead, in the final minutes of her life, she struggles to face the demons of her childhood, involving the death of her father, and in this symbolic battle for her soul, she must decide if she will side with the angels or demons of St. Rosemary's Hospital.

Basically a superior direct-to-DVD release, *Room 6* does many things well but suffers some missteps with other artistic choices. First of all the cast is effective, especially Christine Taylor as haunted heroine Amy, a woman who survives a car crash unharmed, while her boyfriend suffers a broken leg and is rushed to the hospital. However, Amy cannot find the hospital where Nick was rushed, and she joins forces with the survivor of the truck that hit her because his sister, injured, was taken to the same hospital and now both injured parties are missing. Strangely, even though Amy was not physically harmed, she has visions of herself with half her face covered in thick, matted blood, the result of a deep cut on her forehead. And pretty soon her male companion Jerry O'Connell starts to come on to her, and she sees quick flashes of him transformed with a monstrous face. In fact, innocuous homeless people momentarily transform into hideous monsters before reverting to their formerly human selves. Amy's only friends appear to be a little blonde child she councils at school and a benevolent cab driver that always seems to know more than he should.

The movie's climax occurs at St. Rosemary's, a hospital that does not even exist any longer, having burned to the ground years ago. However, the cab driver takes her to the site where the hospital used to be, and then during a thunderstorm, images of the building's façade appear and disappear on each strike of lightning. Amy, terrified of hospitals, has to enter to find her boyfriend, now paralyzed and awake on the operating table, the surgical team ready to sink its scalpel into his chest. But first she has to confront her last hospital experience, when at age 12 she assisted her own father's death, by unplugging him from his life-sustaining machines (by the father's request). Amy, who feels responsible for her father's death, now must relive the entire experience as well as face the more recent demons that have overridden her life. All such horror leads directly back to the automobile crash, but this time it is the boyfriend who is not injured but Amy who is (the flashbacks of her face gorged with blood are the reality of the crash). As her boyfriend tries to get medical help for her, Amy, realizing she is dying, is finally calm and at peace and accepting of her fate as she slips away.

Room 6's strengths, besides its strong performances and clever script, are its sudden flashes of ordinary humans who momentarily morph into zombie burn victims or hideously scarred monstrosities. Also, the claustrophobic strobe-lit sequences of Amy walking down the corridors of St. Rosemary's are quite horrifying. The film's missteps include some directorial choices. Sometimes the monsters linger a frame or two too long or what is forthcoming is telegraphed in too obvious a manner, spoiling the aura of horrific mystery. Jerry O'Connell, the too, too decent guy, suddenly becomes a sleaze bag a little too abruptly. Some of the hospital sets appear to be a little too low rent and the hospital looks unused and too long deserted. The individual patient ward appears too bare-bones. And the hot sexy nurses that are constantly taking blood samples are almost stereotyped, especially during their gratuitous nude blood-bath lesbian sequence where they spray blood all over each other and munch on one of the poor, unfortunate patients. A few sequences feature these same deja-vu visuals that only attest to the fact that the movie has been to the well one time too often. But other sequences are original and quite effective and manage to generate their quota of creepy thrills. *Room 6* is the type of movie that features mediocrity right alongside inspiration, as though the filmmakers haven't gotten their artistic formula quite right. I enjoyed the movie and especially liked Christine Taylor's haunting performance, but too much of Room 6 reminds the viewer of missed potential. But for a lark, the film delivers.

The Hills Have Eyes [Unrated]
Movie: 3.0; Disc: 3.5
Fox

Wes Craven's 1977 horror thriller of the ultimate dysfunctional family was a landmark film of 1970s horror and put Craven's name on the map. The film itself paled compared to <u>Halloween</u> and *Texas Chain Saw Massacre*, but it was a visceral, ultra-gore epic of survival in the American southwestern desert. The film established Michael Berryman as an icon of horror, much in the same way as Rando Hatton became a similar icon a generation earlier. However, Craven's *The Hills Have Eyes* featured only adequate acting and the typically muted, washed out color. The film may have become a classic by virtue of its radiation mutants, on-location photography and ultra gore, but it's a movie that appears low-rent even among other low-rent classics of the era.

Alexandre Aja's remake of *The Hills Have Eyes*, again produced by Wes Craven, is superior in every way to the Craven original by virtue of its more professional photography, better quality professional actors, cutting-edge visual effects and an expanded screenplay.

First of all, Aja's remake appeared to be heading in the wrong direction, with Aja going the *Psycho* remake route and re-filming the earlier film, sequence by sequence, with little originality added to the mix. The opening credits grab the audience's attention immediately, with shots of nuclear testing and explosions juxtaposed against newspaper headlines, with an old Ernest Tubb tune scoring all these festivities. We revision the family's stop at the decaying roadside gas station, their detour off the beaten path and their tires exploding. We revisit the disappearance and mutilation of family dog Beauty, the incineration and tragic death of Big Bob and the invasion of the trailer by the mutant family, resulting in the violent death of Lynn and the rape of Brenda. Déjà vu, yet still superior. While Michael Berryman played a mutant with very little makeup, all the radiation victims here are created by state-of-the-art prosthetics created by Gregory Nicotero and Howard Berger's company and their creations are horrifying and visually intriguing, especially the Big Brain mutant confined to his chair at home. Just remember the sequence in the original where the family members are outside their trailer and they hear a terrible explosive, then see the fire illuminating the nighttime desert. Horrifyingly, their father Big Bob is tied to a tree, which has been set on fire. In the original film this sequence is horrifying and effective. Yet as filmed in the remake, using steady cam, the camera pans left fluidly, locks in on the fire and then the steady cam races full speed toward the flames and the smoldering body, his flesh melting and his pupils turning

white. Punctuated by the bass-booming explosion, the result is a visually arresting sequence that is as horrifying as it is impressive.

However Aja's movie shows its worth in the final quarter when Doug (Aaron Stanford), armed with only a baseball bat and dog Beast, descend upon the Nuclear Testing Village that survived after atomic testing ended, the village abandoned and simply forgotten. Mannequins populate these nuclear test houses, decorated in 1950s décor with pointy-legged furniture and rounded-screen televisions. Doug's goal is to retrieve his kidnapped baby and defeat the mutants. In Craven's original film we hear about atomic testing and see some newspapers, but the action was confined to the desert. Here, we have the similar horrifying desert sequences, but now we have an underground mine where the humans survived the nuclear testing and the testing village where the mutants actually live. During the climactic sequence, Doug fetches his baby, but the father is blind-sided by the seemingly docile mother mutant. Soon bald-headed Pluto, armed with his pickaxe, erupts upon the scene and the resulting chase and battle (Doug barricades the door with a bathtub but Pluto breaks through the side wall unexpectedly) is classic, with furniture being ripped to shreds and Doug bouncing to and fro and running for his life. By the end of his encounter in the village, Doug is bloodier than Bruce Campbell was in *The Evil Dead* and has lost a few finger tips. But he is triumphant and returns to the trailer with his child and dog in hand. However, back at the trailer Papa Jupiter (Billy Drago) is ripping out the chest and eating the heart of dead mother Kathleen Quinlan, when survivors Brenda (Emilie de Raven) and Bobby (Dan Bryd) set a trap using propane that will ignite when Jupiter opens the

trailer door. The resulting explosion is intense.

The only false note is the final sequence. All the survivors are bloodied but happily alive, and while the audience sighs and celebrates the hard-fought happy ending, the camera pans back to reveal mutant eyes looking down at the humans with binoculars, hinting at the *Part II* that may eventually surface. The overwhelming problem of surviving in the desert without a vehicle, dealing with injuries and caring for an infant is trouble enough. Why complicate matters with the threat of more radiated human waste attacking? For the humans, who fought tooth and nail, the ending menace seems simply unfair. Why can't the movie end smply on a triumphant note?

Extras on the disk include an excellent making of documentary, two separate audio commentaries, production diaries and a music video.

High Tension
Movie: 3.5; Disc: 3.5
Lions Gate

Young French director and co-writer Alexandre Aja and creative partner art director, co-writer Gregory Lavasseur, earned so much attention with their French production of Haut Tension (renamed *High Tension* for American release) that the duo graduated to remake Wes Craven's horror classic *The Hills Have Eyes*.

High Tension's reputation preceded its stateside release, the advance word being that this low-budget French production brought fresh blood to the slasher-style horror movie. However, upon American release the film garnered lukewarm reviews, and then even the die-hard horror fans turned against the movie, citing a surprise twist that occurs 13-minutes before the movie's end that absolutely ruins the production. Or, perhaps not!

Boy, so many people simply got it wrong, for *High Tension* is one of the best horror thrillers released during the past decade, and it is stylish as well as visceral. Simply stated, Aja and Lavasseur took the brain-dead slasher subgenre and reinvented it with intelligence and originality, much in the same way that Alfred Hitchcock's *Psycho* reinvented the psychopath genre by also introducing surprising twists that weren't always popular either.

The structure of *High Tension*'s screenplay is essential to its success. The movie begins as battered and sliced heroine Alexia (Maiwenn) sits on a medical table, her bare legs and feet dangling, as she recounts her night of living hell. Instantly the viewer is witness to the young girl running barefoot through the foods, running onto the road and forcing a car to stop, banging on the driver's side window for the unsuspecting man to help her… when she suddenly awakens in the back seat of a car with best friend Marie (Cecile de France), her college study-buddy, driving. The girls are off to the secluded country farm owned by Marie's parents, and the girls plan to spend the weekend studying for exams. Once the girls arrive home, after a terrifying nighttime cornfield sequence, they head to bed when a strange, rusty truck pulls up to the front of the house in the middle of the night. Ringing the doorbell, Marie's father answers the door to be slashed severely with a razorblade by a greasy man wearing mechanic's overhauls. In short succession the father is beheaded, the mother has her throat cut, the younger brother is shot to death with a shotgun while escaping in the cornfield and Marie is bound and chained, as the elusive Alexia evades the serial killer, eventually jumping in the back of the truck with the bound and silent Marie. Stopping at a gas station, Alexia attempts to notify the attendant to call for help, but he is axed to death by the slasher. Alexia steals a car and follows the rusty truck into the woods, the serial killer realizing too soon that he is being followed, so he forces Alexia's car off the road and Alexia and the slasher meet face to face in a battle to the death.

Basic enough plot, right? Ah, the surprise twist makes all the difference.

First of all, hints appear early in the film that things are not as they seem. In the initial sequence where Alexia is tape recording the story, her voice shouts repeatedly: "I won't let anyone come between us anymore." And then there's the physical presence of Alexia herself. In most slasher horror movies, the heroine is sexy and vulnerable, but here Alexia is very androgynous with a close-cropped, mannish haircut and a tight tee that flattens her breasts and offers nary a hint of erotic tease (save for a navel ring). Her initial attitude and tough girl smoking stance casts her immediately as a stereotyped dyke. Alexia chastises Marie for abandoning her at the party last night for three guys. As Alexia drives the car later that night she keeps staring at the sleeping Marie, who orders her to keep her eyes on the road. When she tells Marie about her frantic running in the woods dream, she says, "It was me running after me!" And when the girls arrive at the farmhouse, Alexia takes a smoke and lingers longingly outside the lighted, open bathroom window where Maria is nude and showering. Returning to her room, Alexia slips on her iPod and slips her hand beneath her pants and masturbates to a song about "just another girl."

When we think of slasher films, the personality and distinct identity of the serial killer becomes paramount. Think of the distinction of Jason or Freddy Krueger or the Shape from the Halloween films. Even the recent *Wolf Creek* gained prominence for its folksy Outback slasher, who was a twisted version of Crocodile Dundee. However the fiend here is generic and ordinary. As stated, he is greasy and wears a mechanic's overhauls and a baseball cap with a wide brim, which obscures the top half of his face. Basically we see the killer's nose, cheeks and mouth, but he never changes his non-emotional expression. He's the working class slasher, bland and nondescript. Such a choice of psycho-killer seems ill chosen, but as the movie plays out, there's a rhyme and reason here. Strangely after every family member is brutally slaughtered, Marie is bound (a rubber tube in her mouth with chains and handcuffs securing her) and thrown in the back of the truck (supposedly so the fiend can have fun with her afterwards).

But all of this makes sense when the twist occurs 13 minutes before the end of the movie. In that short period of time the police find the gas station where the rusty truck stopped and they see the attendant dead, an axe buried deeply in his chest. When they replay the surveillance video, instead of the greasy slasher killing the attendant, we see crazed Alexia wielding the axe and killing the male. Remember, Alexia is in custody retelling her story, but the story she tells is all lies. When Alexia finally frees Marie from her bondage, the first words out of her mouth are—"Don't touch me! Get away!"—for Marie saw her friend Alexia slaughter her family. It wasn't some fiend in overhauls.

Many viewers criticize the movie citing the fact that Alexia was in one room with Marie when Marie's brother was shot to death out in the cornfield... how could this be? No, no, no, the cliché where Alexia is actually the slasher mechanic is not in play here. Instead, in her twisted vision, Alexia is retelling the story from her own perspective so she is not the fiend and does not have to occupy the exact space that the mechanic occupied. Alexia is simply obsessed with totally possessing the girl of her dreams, the girl to whom she swears: "I won't let anyone come between us anymore."

High Tension features several standout sequences, all superbly directed and photographed. The initial shortcut through the cornfield at night with the shout of fear... "I think I saw something," prompting the car to stop and both girls to exit and wander aimlessly through the dark rows of corn. It turns out Marie was playing a joke on Alexia, just to frighten her friend, but the tense creepiness is mesmerizing. The slaughter at the farmhouse, methodical and emotionless, is startling with Alexia constantly putting her hand over her mouth to muffle her screaming as she hides under the bed, as the fiend examines her bedroom. And Alexia hides in the wooden-slotted closet as the slasher slits the throat of the mother, whose bulging eyes peer straight ahead inches from where Alexia is hidden. Another clue to Alexia's guilt is based upon the fact that the fiend never once eyeballs Alexia, even though the girl is hopping from one hallway to another room, outside and back, and the killer and intended victim never cross paths. Finally, the sequence in the woods once Alexia's car is smashed resulting in the tense pursuit through the woods is suspense cinema at its most stylish. At last we get to see the mechanical killer without his hat, his face meticulously covered in blood, his eyes bulging. And finally, perhaps the best suspense sequence is the one at the gas station when Alexia first sneaks out of the back of the truck, eyeballing the male attendant in the office, as she tiptoes out of the range of vision of the slasher who is pumping his gas, the dinging increments establishing a powerful sense of punctuated tension. And once the tank is filled and the pinging stops, total suspense has been achieved as Alexia is now hidden in the back of the gas station market (with the terror soon slipping down to the huge bathrooms beneath the station as she now hides in one of the stalls). Bravo to Alexandre Aja.

With only two horror films to his credit, Alexandre Aja has established a distinct style. He enjoys car destruction and victims being trapped within fiery vehicles. Secondly, influenced by Sam Raimi, Aja enjoys showing the faces of fiends and victims being covered in well-designed blood. Aja enjoys weapons that penetrate the human body (too many to mention from *The Hills Have Eyes*; Marie's metal piercing of Alexia's body at the end of *High Tension* stands out). Aja enjoys protracted Val Lewton–style walks where innocent victims are carefully followed as they venture forth into a mundane setting that quickly becomes the scene of terror (the desert wanderings in *The Hills Have Eyes*; the cornfield sequence in *High Tension*). And in both movies sexuality becomes a reason for slaughter.

Extras include several ex-cellent documentaries, audio commentaries, an unrated English-language dubbed version (nicely done) and the original French language director's cut. At this point in time I would never believe that someone could reinvent the slasher film with innovation and creativity, but this is exactly what Aja has done. If anyone feels put off by the shocking revelation near the film's end and the turn-about and surprise twist, just remember the sight of Anthony Perkins wearing his mother's clothing, his wig falling off, as he sits in the police headquarters staring silently as psycho-babble is voiced over the soundtrack explaining what exactly occurred in Norman Bates' mind to make him a killer. Examined in isolation, that gimmicky twist seems ridiculous and silly, but taken in the total framework of the movie, the twist is a beautiful one. The same logic applies to *High Tension*. Deal with it!

Demon Hunter
Movie: 2.0; Disc: 3.5
Anchor Bay

The direct-to-video market has become the B film of the modern era, and sometimes the filmmakers do a better-than-average job with films such as Room 6. However, *Demon Hunter* is typically bland horror by the numbers, with a few glimmers of creativity.

First, the opening exorcism sequence involving Lea Moreno Young (Maria) is one of the surprises. She plays the demon-possessed young lady who playfully seduces the priest who is conducting the exorcism, and when Sean Patrick Flanery (Jake) enters the room to find the priest dead ("Hello, pretty man. Are you here for your friend? I'm afraid you're too late to save him."), the sexy nightgown clad devil pulls up her gown and asks Jake, "Do you want to play with me." Then in a terrific battle sequence, the demon flies across the room and Jake and Maria have a fight to the death. A very exciting beginning.

Jake is a half-breed, a spawn of a demon and human, who works for the Catholic Church. He comes in to destroy demons when an exorcism fails. Jake's superior is Cardinal White (William Bassett), a mysterious man who proves to be just as cold-hearted and ruthless as the demons the church is fighting. He is assigned a beautiful young nun, Sister Sarah (Colleen Porch), to become his moral compass and help him in his assignment. The sister, herself raised by the church, has a dark past which becomes exposed by the movie's end. Jake's assignment is to destroy Asmodeus (Billy Drago), the demon of seduction, who has been impregnating hookers all over town. Drago's performance is perhaps the best in the movie, looking frail and handsome in a past-your-prime way. Asmodeus sports vampire fangs and is constantly photographed in bed with naked women surrounding him. Amodeus' assistant is the Succubus (Tania Deighton), a seductive half-dressed demon sporting devil's horns, whose mission is to seduce the innocent to evil. However, Jake, whose what-the-hell attitude allows him to flirt with the dark side, willfully allows this demon of sexuality to have her way with him, and he manages to get the upper hand at the same time.

The movie meanders with a very predictable plot, Kung-Fu fighting, hidden lairs and a brooding hero who is unsure whose side he should fight for. Sister Sarah's transformation at the end is not really much of a surprise, but their climatic duel to the death between two tainted heroes working for the church is very interesting.

Producer Stephen J. Cannell obviously intended *Demon Hunter* to be the start of a series, and it still might sire a sequel or two. However, *Demon Hunter* smacks too much of been there, done that to be worthy of a repeated offering. Flanery's character of Jake is our typical anti-hero who, like Wesney Snipes in Blade, is fighting to maintain his humanity while battling the dark side. Flanery's Jake is a tad too off-putting and lethargic for my own liking, and he never seems happy or satisfied by what he does. It's almost as if he secretly yearns to be killed in his noble battle to be put out of his misery. The film is worth a watch, but just barely.

The Witch's Mirror
Movie: 3.0; Disc: 3.5
CasaNegra

A few years ago Image Entertainment announced they would inaugurate individual releases of the classic Mexican horror movies produced from the 1950s through the 1960s, all of which came directly to television in goofy dubbed versions masterminded by K. Gordon Murray. Quite abruptly after Image's initial release, the company announced the series had to be aborted, because of a rights issue. For too brief a time, Spanish DVD distributor CasaNegra emerged to carry on the legacy of releasing many

Mexican horror chillers, before bankruptcy put them under in only a few short years. These releases will contain the uncut Spanish language versions (K. Gordon Murray usually cut at least 5 minutes from the original print) in both a Spanish language with English subtitled version, or, for the purist, the K. Gordon Murray original English dubbed versions (with the restored cut sequences only in Spanish). The CasaNegra prints used and mastered are superior to the TV released 16mm K. Gordon Murray prints. These remastered 35mm prints blow the old TV prints away. However, *The Witch's Mirror* digital print frequently contains sequences of faces that have a slight glow, as if the print were printed slightly overexposed. Such a flaw does not ruin the film experience, but the glow is noticeable and slightly annoying when the presentation otherwise is flawless, without any noticeable splices, scratches or flaws.

CasaNegra's initial release, surprisingly, is not one of their highly regarded vampire movies but the first of their witch series. Mexican horror icon Abel Salazar produces and Chano Ureuta (*The Brainiac*) directs. The decaying and ornate set decoration is created by Dario Cabanas, while Jorge J. Stahl lenses the moody cinematography. What these Mexican horror movies create is an unique Euro black-and-white air of disease and undead. Sometimes the screenplay and acting suffers, but at their best these Mexican films create a tableau that equals what Mario Bava and Terence Fisher did so well... create grand art direction on a budget. In fact *The Witch's Mirror* most resembles the Euro-Italian horror movies of the 1960s, and at its best, mimics the style of Mario Bava. Even the plot resembles the typical Barbara Steele horror revenge tale that she made so famous.

Here, elderly mother witch Sarah (Isabela Corona) looks into her full-length magic mirror and sees her doctor son-in-law Eduardo (Armando Calvo) plot the death of beautiful daughter Elena (Dina De Marco), because he now loves another woman, Deborah (Rosita Arenas), and wishes his freedom. In protracted, moody opening sequences, looks and gestures say it all as Elena plays morbid songs at her piano. Eduardo prepares warm milk for Elena at bedtime, and the cautious wife hesitates before drinking and then asks her husband why he hates her so. Without answering, the wife falls dead on her bed, but shortly thereafter her witch mother attempts to make a pact with the devil to spare her daughter, but to no avail. Destiny must be carried out. However, mother Sarah uses her powers to raise the ghost of Elena from the dead, and together, both women plot their revenge.

What makes *The Witch's Mirror* such a wonderful movie is its surreal and foreboding mood. Strangley, the grave of Elena with its exposed casket is never covered over with earth, and a ghostly white-robed figure emerges to haunt the castle and its evil inhabitants. In a climactic sequence near the film's middle, the witch's mirror is broken and the room erupts into an inferno, flames that burn and scar the face and arms of beautiful Deborah, and the doctor spends the remainder of the film, in typical *Eyes Without a Face* manner, abducting beautiful young women and using their skin as grafts to restore the beautiful face of his lover. But the surreal touches stand front and center. In one sequence the ghostly Elena literally drops both of her hands on the doctor's table, allowing him to graft his former wife's hands onto the stumps of Deborah. Of course, influenced by *The Hands of Orlac*, Deborah cannot control the impulses of such hands that ultimately attempt to strangle her husband. While the bevy of beautiful young victims results in the total restoration of Deborah's beauty, in the film's final minute her new expressive hands rot and fall from her arms and her face returns to its horribly burned state. Again, similar to Italian horror films of the period, the plot is bare bones and only presents a haunting excuse for supernatural revenge. But *The Witch's Mirror* offers grisly makeup and moody direction with an abundance of the surreal. Style over substance, but in the case of this type of movie, style becomes substance and audiences can cut the dense mood with a knife. *The Witch's Mirror* is not the best of what is to come, but it is most definitely an exciting debut for the short-lived series.

The Curse of the Crying Woman
Movie: 3.0; Disc: 3.5
CasaNegra

Of the initial two Casa Negra Mexican horror releases, *The Curse of the Crying Woman* is the superior movie, but once again its similarity to The Witch's Mirror becomes apparent immediately. Both films use a mirror as a central, haunting image. Both films feature disfigured women. Both films involve the resurrection of a dead woman for purposes of revenge. Abel Salazar produces both movies and each film stars Rosita Arenas. And most spectacularly, both films create a sense of Gothic unease with oppressive layers of haunting mood accentuating every sequence. And never have these Mexican productions looked this good.

Rafael Baledon directs in a style similar to Chano Urueta, but the screenplay offers a tighter, more expansive script (co-written by the director), and the film's budget offers a better production look and more elaborate set pieces.

The story involves young Amelia (Rosita Arenas), who with her husband Jaime (Abel Salazar), journeys to visit her mysterious Aunt Selma (Rita Macedo), who lives alone with spooky servants in her isolated castle. One crazed servant slaughters passengers of a carriage traveling through the nearby woods in the film's opening sequence, so the audience is very much aware that Aunt Selma is also an evil witch. As the story develops we discover that the rotting corpse of an old woman chained to a wheel with a lance piercing her heart, is the mother of Aunt Selma and that Amelia, the last in the line of descendants, is predestined to remove the stake restoring the elder witch to full life and power. Of course Amelia is unaware of such a mission until the film's final act.

The film's major sequences involve Aunt Selma appearing as the crying woman, her own eyes reconstructed as bulging black orbs, which make her impossible to distinguish as Aunt Selma. Selma's husband, similar to the Richard Wordsworth character in Hammer's Curse of the Werewolf, is locked away in the bell tower (a wonderful and haunting set piece) prison, half mad and more animalistic than human. When Amelia wanders up the long and foreboding tower steps, she gazes in amazement at the top, backing nearer and nearer the dark cell from where two claw-like hands emerge. In other masterful sequences, as the time gets nearer for the corpse in the basement to be reanimated, the cinematographer Jose Ortiz Ramos creates double-exposures layering the crusty corpse with glimpses of the same corpse now alive with open eyes. As the lance is slowly pulled out, the layer showing the living corpse becomes more visually dominant than the original rotting, dead corpse. Such sequences again add a surreal touch. The Mexican reliance upon supernatural occurrences elevates their Gothic style.

Strong and silent, Abel Salazar becomes a dominant presence and a hero of distinction. Whether he is using coiled rope to flatten the wire-flung rubber bats or avoiding crumpling stones and rocks during the films's climax, he is a man on whom one can rely. The exciting climax, with the decaying house literally cracking and imploding upon the inhabitants, benefits from the film's budget. In the money shot, the evil, crippled servant looks up and sees the metal bell break loose from its housing and tumble downward. However, instead of a grand sequence showing the evil servant crushed by the heavy bell, the bell lands on top of already fallen beams and lumber, crushing the servant in a far less dramatic way.

The Curse of the Crying Woman is very evocative of the visual style of Black Sunday, Mario Bava's classic. In fact, the film begins with the witchy black-orbed crying woman standing near the stopped carriage, holding three Great Danes in hand, a sequence mirroring the similar sequence from *Black Sunday,* with the hauntingly beautiful Barbara Steele holding the leash of large dogs. To be quite honest, any film that uses *Black Sunday* as its inspiration is headed in the right artistic direction. Once again the cinematography and art direction shine, and the cast does a more than adequate job, especially Rosita Arenas as Amelia and Rita Macedo as Aunt Selma. The movie is never dull, with enough mood, supernatural occurrences and suspense to keep everyone focused.

Extras include an audio commentary, full color booklet, a colorful card game, onscreen essay on the director, cast bios and a poster and still gallery. These CasaNegra discs are worth collecting and once again remind us that the United States and England weren't the only countries making impressive horror movies during the 1950s and 1960s.

Skeleton Key
Movie: 3.0; Disc: 3.5
Universal

The major complaint about the modern horror movie is that unrelenting pacing and an over-abudance of CGI effects dominate story and character. Another common complaint is the lack of atmospherically generated chills. Well, surprise, *Skeleton Key* is guilty of being almost exactly the opposite, its Southern Gothic adult approach is almost too atmospheric and slow-building for its own good (most voodoo movies are guilty of lethargic pacing). The cast exudes class: Gena Rowlands, John Hurt and even Kate Hudson bring a commitment to creating complex characterizations that are seldom found in the modern horror movie. The production detail and cinematographer also raise the creative bar. The script by Ehren Kruger (the American *Ring* series and *The Brothers Grimm*) and the direction by Iain Softley (*K-Pax*) bear the bulk of the problems. Kruger's script, like M. Night Shyamalan's for *The Sixth Sense*, features a shocking gimmicky ending. The movie reads almost as if Kruger came up with the clever ending first and tried to write a script around it. The overall script suffers when one of the major characters, who appears to be a good person, is revealed to be in cahoots with evil. *The Sixth Sense*, although based upon the same shocking type of gimmick, simply has more meat on the bone, more substance, and the movie stands on its own, even without the ending. Here, Kruger has created a modern equivalent of the equally Southern Gothic *Hush, Hush, Sweet Charlotte*, where cinematography and mood substitute for plot. And while the acting goes a long way to maintain focus and interest, too little occurs with Softley failing to duplicate the Gothic, ghostly mood of far better productions such as *The Haunting* (1960) or *The Innocents*. The audience jumps, but not often enough. Softley does not wish to veer into the supernatural domain until the film's very ending; instead, he opts for locked attic rooms, unexplained footsteps and voodoo imagery. If Softley can be accused of any flaw, it is simply he appears afraid to make *Skeleton Key* a balls out horror exercise in mood and horror. The director plays things too safe.

The story involves a married black couple, servants of course, who lived in the attic room of the mansion 90 years earlier. The servant couple were proponents of hoodoo magic. During a party, the owner's children vanish and are found up in the attic room with the servants, some type of spell supposedly being cast over them. The black servants are immediately lynched on the front lawn and their bodies set on fire. The two children, brother and sister, remain in the house until the current owner Violet (Gena Rowlands) buys the house (or so she claims) in 1962 and lives there with her husband Ben (John Hurt). The too-serious Caroline (Kate  Hudson) accepts a job to be a live-in hospice caretaker for Ben, who has suffered a massive stroke and is expected to linger for another month or so. However, almost immediately Ben, mostly with his fearful eyes, conveys to Caroline that he has not been stricken by a stroke and that hoodoo magic and spells are the cause of his malady. As Caroline is educated slowly in the ways of the Old South and clandestine hoodoo shops, she begins to believe that things at the estate are not as they seem and that the spirit of the long-dead black servants permeate the house and the occupants within.

The surprise ending, not to be revealed here, is totally unsatisfying because the film ends on such a depressing note that audiences feel cheated. Caroline, who is guilt-ridden over abandoning her father during his final fatal illness, has become a hospice worker, a truly caring one, who tries to make up past failings by doing for others what she failed to do for her own father. Caroline literally goes through Hell to help the seemingly cursed Ben and risks her life to help cure him. Ben, in a similar fashion, begins to respond to Caroline's charms and spells and even regains his speech partially. The movie's plot is basically Caroline's journey to reconcile the flaws of the past with her new-found strength at the moment, and such heroic and noble growth should never be rewarded by the downbeat fate she suffers at the film's end. Ben too, so heroic and

noble in his fight, is equally defeated. *Skeleton Key* is an adult counterpart to all the 1980s slasher movies (created in the wake of *Carrie*) where evil wins and innocence is corrupted. To me *Skeleton Key*'s ending is just as false and unsatisfying as those 1980s movies with their equally depressing endings. Yes, the gimmick is a clever one and makes for a horrifying and chilling climax, but the fate of the two decent characters ruins everything.

Extras included are marvelous, including audio commentary, and several documentaries explaining the difference between voodoo and hoodoo.

May
Movie: 3.0; Disc: 3.5
Lions Gate

Watching *Sick Girl* from *The Masters of Horror* DVD and really enjoying the direction of Lucky McKee and the acting of Angela Bettis, I decided to go back to 2002 and watch the movie that created the buzz for both (that and the TV remake of *Carrie*, also in 2002, which starred Bettis). Reading about *May* for a few years now, I was glad I actually took the time to catch up. Directed and written by Lucky McKee and starring Angela Bettis as the title character, May becomes Carrie for this generation. Like Carrie the young women has the challenge to raise above her lazy eye and eye patch and suffer the heartbreak of corrective lenses and appearing different. But as a young woman who lives in an apartment on her own, though shy, May can cope and interact with others. In fact at her job at the animal clinic as assistant veterinarian, she makes friends with a zany girl Polly (Anna Faris), a lesbian that hits on May, and May, looking for love anywhere she can find it, begins to experiment with her sexuality until she discovers Polly cheating on her. May pursues a guy that she thinks possesses the perfect hands, and she begins to follow him around and eat in the same places that he does, hoping that he will notice her. But Adam (Jeremy Sisto) simply reads while he eats and dozes off. In one poignant sequence, while Adam sleeps, May bends over him and allows his dangling hand to brush against her cheeks and she imagines what it would be like to be caressed by a fully awake boyfriend. Suddenly, Adam awakes and the two start to date, even though Adam finds May a tad too weird for his own horror film splatter tastes. While showing May his short zombie movie where a victim's finger is nibbled off, she offers critical insight that the zombie would not devour the entire finger so quickly. And when bleeding from the lip, May thinks his kissing her bloody face would be a turn on, but the young man is far less kinky than the willing-to-do-anything May. When Adam stops phoning May, May hovers outside his home and front door for hours, waiting for him to leave the house so he will have to make contact. Persistent yet weird, May is looking for friendship in all the wrong ways. At her home her only friend is a special big-eyed weird doll that her mother gave her, and the doll, not to be touched, is encased in glass. As May descends into madness, the glass housing her insulated friend begins to crack, as though strained by May's bouts of anger and depression.

In my humble opinion, Lucky McKee wanted to make an alienation movie, a "chick flick" for the estranged generation. In fact for most of the film we are not anywhere near horror movie land. The horror aspects seem to imply May's only solution to having friends, by way of her mother's advice. Her mom told May, to have friends you have to make them, and with this she gave May her glass encased doll. For the dispirited young woman who tries so hard to connect with other people, sexual orientation not a problem, she remembers these words from her past, and sets out to create the perfect friend, anatomically piece by piece. Just like Dr. Frankenstein, she can use Adam's hands, her one good eye (self mutilation is one means that May is able to release the pressure inside), etc. So May devolves into the ritualistic serial killer, the forsaken misfit that will create a friend by any means possible. Yet May's alienation becomes a dominant theme.

Volunteering to assist young blind children at a special school, May takes her only friend, her doll, to show the children, and when they break the case and destroy the doll, this becomes the final straw that snaps her sanity and makes her delusional and psychotic. When the film reverts to mayhem, gore and splatter, the film's shortcomings surface, and Lucky McKee appears to have made such concessions only to win distribution on the B-horror film circuit. His heart and head is focused mainly on the inner psychology of his title character May, the bloodshed and murder seems only a necessary evil. His is definitely a character study of a troubled girl, and with such a wonderful script and a stellar break-out performance, it is amazing that star Angela Bettis has not risen to the top immediately, for her performance is incredible. In the film's early sequences with her askew eye, she looks about 12 years old. For most of the film she looks about 19 or 20, and by the ending, once she applies her cosmetics, she looks mid-20s. And whether she is Gothed out or glammed up, Bettis is totally believable in a performance that touches the heart. Even though the horror trappings seem superfluous, they may very well be necessary to show May's choices once things go wrong and her circuits become hot-wired. Anyway, with *Sick Girl* and *May*, Lucky McKee demonstrates a potential talent worth nurturing. And if there's any justice left in Hollywood, Angela Bettis should also be a rising young star.

The Stendhal Syndrome
Movie: 3.0; Disc: 3.5
Troma

Many people thought that Dario Argento lost his touch after *Opera*, made during the mid-1980s, but his recent movies produced during the past 20 years have held up better than anticipated. Anchor Bay releases of *The Card Player* and Trauma and Troma's (more recently Blue Underground's) release of 1996's *The Stendhal Syndrome* prove otherwise. The 1970s of course remain the golden period for Argento and his absolute best work was produced during that decade, but his more recent work deserves credit as well.

The Stendhal Syndrome is one trippy horror movie, starring Argento's daughter Asia, who always seems to be naked or molested in each of her father's films. In this film Asia, looking sensual yet hard and somewhat unsymmetrical, sports deep lines under both eyes. She plays a police detective on the trail of a rapist/murderer and she finds herself the victim.

The film's first 25 minute sequence is a surreal and dream-like classic, showing the affects of police detective Anna Manni (Asia Argento) suffering from the Stendhal Syndrome, a psychological disorder where Manni becomes trancelike walking through an Italian art museum, the great works of art making Manni disoriented and dizzy. The frail woman collapses, cutting her lip in the fall. During such seizures Manni hears the art talk, or a painting's threatening countenance becomes threatening to only her. The young man who helps Manni fetch a cab, returns in this phantasmagoric dream moments later. First Manni, suffering from amnesia, returns to her apartment and learns her name from a prescription in her purse. Looking at a painting hanging on her apartment wall, the art distorts and fades as Anna walks directly into the painting. Now interacting in the painting which becomes her reality, the police detective investigates a murder scene, the 15th rape victim becomes the first victim to be murdered by the serial fiend. Manni is put on the case but immediately the young man who helped her at the museum returns now as the serial rapist, who uses a razor produced from his mouth to cut her lip, thus arousing him after kissing the bleeding lips, and he rapes her.

In the midst of her own rape she envisions the same man raping another victim, this time shooting the screaming victim through the mouth (the slo-mo cinematography shows the bullet penetrate and exit from the woman's mouth leaving a gapping hole). Manni is next seen at the hospital being examined and given a sedative, yet she is left alone and uses scissors left on the table to cut off her long hair, creating a new persona for herself. Like the beginning to Brian De Palma's *Dressed to Kill*, Argento's *Stendhal Syndrome* opens with almost pure visuals that are both dreamlike, druggy yet horrifyingly realistic. The reality of Manni's situation is driven home by surreal imagery, so in the hands of master Argento, the narrative and horrifying imagery work together to tell the tale.

In another quirky sequence, Anna's boyfriend, trying to arouse in her the old erotic feelings of old, finds Anna to have changed, to hate the thought of sex, and in an abrupt about-face, Anna begins to talk dirty, physically abuse her boyfriend, force him to turn his face to the wall as she undoes his pants and fondles him in a most unwilling manner, causing the boyfriend to fall to the floor sobbing. Memories of her rape are too debilitating for Anna to surmount, and in a turnabout moment, Anna molests and humiliates her lover sexually just as she has been during her own rape. Anna is not her self and needs therapy, which she does pursue.

Defying police protection provided for Anna, the rapist/murderer manages to apprehend Anna once again, taking her to a torture chamber surrounded by demented art, typing her to a mattress and having his way with her, this time using his razor blade to slice the side of her face. Leaving her tied to the mattress, the fiend returns later that evening to find the police woman ready for him, as Anna stabs him in the neck and kicks him repeatedly, using a freed mattress spring to gouge his eye out, until she grabs his gun and shoots him point blank, but he remains on his feet until Anna continues to beat him senseless. Anna continues to taunt and kick the half-dead molester, but instead of allowing the police to apprehend what's left of him, Anna kicks him down a waterfalls canal system. In Argentoland, he may very well survive.

In the final act of the film, Anna now dons a blonde wig to create a still different persona, befriends a new young man, and discovers that he is a professor at an art museum. Of course the climax occurs there, amidst all the paintings and statues forming a fantastic, horrific set piece to any victim suffering from the Stendhal Syndrome. In the midst of horror, the young professor is shot dead by an unseen assassin.

Asia Argento steals the film with her riveting performance. Argento, sensual but not actually sexy, plays so many moods effectively: the dedicated police detective, the defenseless rape victim, the spiteful woman scorned, the sexual aggressor, the beautiful victim, the drugged-out victim of a psychological disorder, the fearful woman, the empowered woman. She becomes the film's centerpiece and the entire plot, all its imagery, is centered around her disturbed character, a character of great strength, even when victimized by men, art, amorous boyfriends and herself (Anna admits to herpsychiatrist that she cuts herself to feel better).

Ennio Morricone provides the intense musical score that enhances the moody cinematography by Giuseppe Rotunno. Several excellent documentaries are included including Lloyd Kaufman's interview with Dario Argento (though both are never in the same room at the same time... humm).

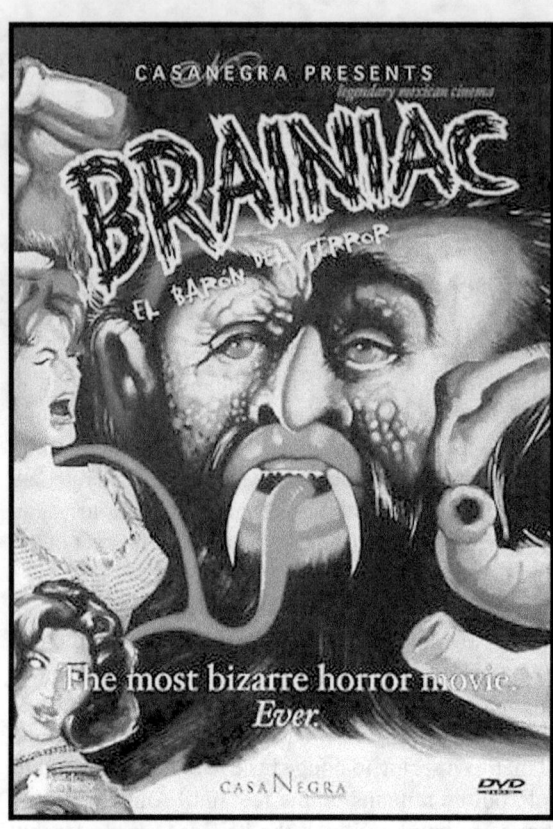

The Brainiac
Movie: 3.0; Disc: 3.5
CasaNegra

CasaNegra releases of Mexican horror movies, available in the uncut Spanish language/English subtitled editions, and where applicable, the edited-down K. Gordon Murry redubbed version, continue with this cult favorite.

Popular and weird, *The Brainiac* appears beautifully remastered in a video print that avoids the flaring contrast that marred the initial two releases (*The Witch's Mirror* and *Curse of the Crying Woman*). In this Chano Urueta-directed quirky classic, produced by and starring Abel Salazar, *The Brainiac* becomes the Mexican equivalent of the best cinema of Ed Wood, Jr. If anything, *The Brainiac* has chutzpah and the energy to pull it off. Salazar plays an evil Baron judged by the Inquisition for his evil acts in 1661 and condemned to burn at the stake. As the superimposed flames lick higher a comet appears in the night skies. The Baron announces that when the comet returns again in 300 years (1961 to be exact), he will inflict his revenge on all the heirs of those who condemned him.

The movie is populated with obvious rear screen projection shots to approximate location shooting, and such cheap shortcuts become one of the film's most charming aspects. When a papier-mâché comet literally plops onto the soundstage, the spirit of the now reincarnated Baron possesses a pathetic victim unlucky enough to be on the scene. In his most evil guise, that of The Brianiac, the Baron morphs into a rubber-headed demon with undulating mask that compresses and expands and a yardstick-long forked tongue becomes erect and rises from his mouth, penetrating the backs of his victim's head. In a low-rent special effect, he supposedly sucks out the brains of his victims, and he stores the brains in an ornate metal dish locked in a wooden chest that he visits frequently for midnight snacking. Unlike *Fiend Without a Face*, we do not see any gooey slurping, just the attachment of the elongated tongue to the backs of the neck with two vampiric puncture holes as proof of the insidious attacks. In a crazy sequence, the distinguished Baron (Salazar) lures German Robles (goateed and bug-eyed) and his lady friend away from other party guests when he transforms into the gruesome Brianiac. As the Robles character stands paralyzed with fear, the Brainiac fondles and kisses the zombified lady friend before going in for the kill, just another way to torture his victims and exert his power. Several such sequences occur that are as audacious as they are silly. But because of the intensity by which they are delivered, such hokeyness succeeds.

As the Baron tracks down the descendants of those Inquisition judges who condemned him to death (in his eyes the faces of those modern people are momentarily replaced by their ancient hooded counterparts), the tension grows as the Baron becomes a serial brain-stealing fiend, yet no one suspects his guilt, because of his prominence and respectability. Once again the film is aided by the use of large and ornate Gothic sets that are dressed to chilling perfection. The sight of a distinguished Abel Salazar morphing into a man with a rubber mask and ridiculously long tongue should be the dramatic kiss of death, yet somehow such shenanigans draw the viewer's attention, not repel it. *The Brainiac* might be one of the most silly and far-fetched low-budget productions ever, yet its Hammer-style acting where no one dares wink or smile only intensifies the corresponding lush sets and brilliant directorial mood. Perhaps such overkill succeeds because the movie is Mexican and subsequently subtitled/dubbed. Perhaps the suspension of disbelief is heightened because *The Brianiac* is not American made. But while *The Brainiac* is not a classic and never tries to be more than a fun-filled exploitation romp, the film manages to succeed on this level and remains one of the most beloved cult classics of its time.

Extras include audio commentary, a documentary, an Interactive Digital Press Kit, an original American radio spot ad, a colorful card game, cast and crew bios and a poster and still gallery. But most exceptionally is the wonderfully remastered video print that returns The Brianiac to theatrical quality excellence.

Jenifer: [*Masters of Horror* Showtime]
Movie: 3.0; Disc: 3.5
Anchor Bay

The more I see of the *Masters of Horror* Showtime anthology series, the more I am impressed. Simply for returning the work of Italian maestro Dario Argento to mainstream television, the series deserves praise. And Argento's contribution to the first season, *Jenifer* (based upon a cult comic of the 1970s and scripted by star Steven Weber), is a delight that blends eroticism and horror in equal doses. Even though scored by frequent collaborator Claudio Simonetti (formerly of Goblin), Jenifer does not resemble the typical Argento film. The camera movement seems pedestrian (except for a wild, over-the-top-from-the-ceiling-looking-down sequence, while the naked Jenifer straddles Weber in bed) and the visuals fail to approximate Argento's standard dream reality. However, Argento's style, here Americanized, does produce startling effects. The little known Carrie Anne Fleming portrays a mentally challenged and disfigured mute girl (her eyes contain totally black pupils, her mouth is twisted and elongated exposing savage animal teeth and her face is askew and scaly); however, from the neck down she is built like the proverbial brick shithouse, reminding male viewers of the old sexist adage: put a paper paper bag over her head!

The story deals with sexual obsession and how a manipulative cannibalistic girl can destroy the lives of men, easily at will. The hour teleplay begins with cop Weber tak-

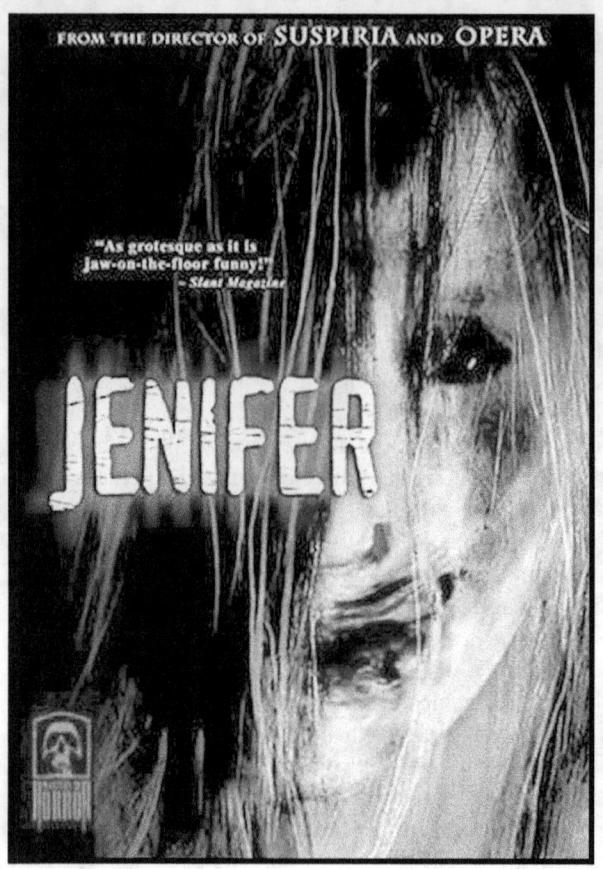

ing a break with his partner near a deserted wooded area near the water. One strange pervert is leading a barely dressed woman down a path, ready to slice-and-dice her, when Weber fires his weapon stopping the murder in mid-air. Once he sees the face of the intended victim, now bent over a barrel, he is shocked by the victim's unfortunate looks, but the mute victim cuddles and appreciates that her life has been spared. The homeless unfortunate is admitted to a mental hospital where Weber checks on her while she is showering. She exits, wearing only a towel and has nothing but hugs and kisses to give her handsome rescuer. Before long, and this is where the plot strains credibility, Weber signs the girl's release and brings her home to sleep on the couch. As she lies there half-naked with one breast exposed, Weber's excited teenage son comments that she has a great rack. Before long Jenifer literally eats their pet cat and the wife and son storm out in a cab, never to return. Jenifer has been showing her gratitude by seducing and having sex with Weber in his family car, and such extracted sequences sizzle. Weber moves with Jenifer to a run-down mountain cabin: he becomes an unemployed drunk, soon resembling the pervert he killed in the story's opening minutes. The cannibalistic Jenifer attacks, kills and eats innocent victims, then strangely she changes into the cuddling sex kitten that satisfies Weber's desires. The ending is predicable as hell, but the overall comic book-come-to-life is quite satisfying in an hour setting.

Argento's nouveau style merging the bestial and the beautiful embarks upon some themes brand new to his work; however, the erotic side of horror is always front and center, and Jenifer's zombie-like glee as she tears with her teeth into an adolescent's ribcage and groin (a sequence where she eats his erect penis is detailed in the accompanying documentary, but was, of course, cut out from the final version, thank god) is akin to her lust for Weber in a more conventional, physical way. Sequences of over-the-top splatter (cat slaughter, entrails being consumed) seem overdone and draw too much attention to themselves, but the kinetic energy that Fleming brings to her performance as Jenifer is feral, audacious and wild… she really becomes this female sensual creature whose cannibalistic yearnings to feed become more animalistic than savage. Yet Weber's sexual obsession with such a horrible creature does strain credibility. So while Weber's screenplay is problematic, all the major performances are multi-layered, rich and interesting. However, in such a short movie, Weber's spiritual and physical deterioration from proud cop to derelict is not properly motivated.

Flawed, embarrassingly perverse and quirky, Argento's *Jenifer* bursts with directorial energy and passion and offers many new reasons for women to hate the now veteran horror film director.

The Black Pit of Dr. M
Movie: 3.0; Disc: 3.5
CasaNegra

Contrary to popular belief, K. Gordon Murray did not dub all the best Mexican horror movies, because *The Black Pit of Dr. M* was a Mexican horror movie released theatrically and was not included in Murray's renowned television package. In many ways *Mysteries from Beyond the Grave* (the literal American translation of the Mexican title and a far better title than the exploitative release title) might be the best Gothic Mexican movie of them all, directed in 1959 by Fernando Mendez (who also directed *The Vampire* and *The Vampire's Coffin*). The movie is evocative of Mario Bava's *Black Sunday,* with similar cinematography and mood permeating both productions.

The story is straight out of H.P. Lovecraft. Two doctors swear that the first to die will come back and allow the other to experience death, without actually dying (a nifty trick to accomplish). Dr. Aldama is the first to die, and after his death, he returns momentarily to tell Dr. Mazali that in three months, on a specific day, a door will close and seal his fate. He will have his wish, but at a great cost. Aldama is very mysterious and seems to be trying to warn Mazali from pursuing his intended wishes. Soon Al-dama visits his estranged daughter and gives her a key and tells her to go see Dr. Mazali and he will have the box this key will open. Of course this is all connected to Mazali's fate. Add to the mix Elmer, the hospital orderly, whose disfigured face will feature prominently into the Gothic mix.

First of all, the screenplay by Ramon Obon is complex and becomes more of a mystery plot where all the pieces seem to be introduced haphazardly. But they all end up fitting together to produce a satisfying, if depressing, conclusion. We know that Mazali wants to experience death yet wants to also live beyond the posted crossover date three months from now. Mazali works as the doctor at a mental institution, and the prime patient is known as the Gypsy, a middle-aged woman who becomes violent and destructive. In her rage she tosses furniture across the examining room and throws acid into poor Elmer's face (when he heals and he first sees his disfigured face, he almost becomes as violent as her). Only the tune of the music box can keep her calm, but when the woman slams the box shut stopping the music, she becomes crazed within seconds. Her sequence of combative fury is produced way over the top, with all the men in attendance appearing powerless to capture her. However, in spite of the potential for camp, this sequence is gripping with the tension leading to the disfiguring acid bath climax. Even more effective are the course of events on the fateful day where Elmer finally gets his revenge by using a letter opener to stab the Gypsy to death, but he escapes

and the French doors shut eerily as the woman dies in the arms of Dr. Mazali. When the doors reopen, the collected people who enter the room all think that Mazali is the murder, and he is immediately arrested, tried, sentenced and executed. However, in the meantime, Elmer has committed suicide and is buried in a too shallow grave. Of course, at the time of Mazali's death by hanging, his soul is transferred into Elmer's body, a body that becomes resurrected and emerges, worse for wear, from the grave. The climatic ending is a hoot.

Watching the movie in Mexican with American subtitles is the only way to watch it, and the film seldom becomes silly or comical. The cinematography by Victor Herrera anchored by the keen direction by Mendez, together with the pounding repetitive score by Gustavo Cesar Carrion, make for a well-crafted horror chiller whose plot and keen characterization draw the spectator into all the ghostly festivities. The chilling asylum setting with the fog-shrouded garden exterior provides a suspenseful backdrop. In one frightening sequence, the Gypsy is wandering around the outside of the asylum, hiding in the bushes, when Aldama's daughter goes to knock on Mazali's private quarters. Just as the disturbed woman creeps up behind the unaware victim, activity inside the building frightens the fiend away. Sequences of corpses emerging from freshly dug graves impress, ghostly occurrences including objects that appear magically and doors that slam shut due to ghostly intervention are creepy, as are the nocturnal visits from the now dead Dr. Aldama, when he comes visiting during the bewitching hours. A rather well executed plot added to such sequences of Gothic suspense make *The Black Pit of Dr. M* one of the best Mexican horror movies made, and while it pales when compared to the best of Bava, *Black Pit of Dr. M* becomes one more excellent foreign entry awaiting rediscovery via its DVD release. The extras, which are many, include bios of cast and crew, still and poster gallery, printed essays and a music video made to honor the movie. I for one never saw this movie upon its American drive-in release during the early 1960s, but after seeing this pristine and dense DVD release, uncut, and released in its original language, I am sorry I missed it the first time around.

Editor's Note: This is our catch-up issue, so forgive some reviews here of titles released two years ago! As we attempt to return to our regular twice-a-year schedule (not there yet), the reviews will become more and more current.

Grave Diggings

Dear Gary and Sue:

I have to praise you both for the latest issue of *Midnight Marquee*. It is absolutely beautiful from the front cover to the back cover. And the contents are all extremely interesting. I especially liked the Forum/Against 'Em article on *The Wolf Man*. I have read this three times already and the opinions of everyone are so insightful that I had to watch the movie again to see whose side I was on. Quite honestly, I seem to be somewhere in the middle, as wishy-washy as that may sound.

I like the movie but I agree that it does have flaws. I don't want to dump on Chaney, Jr. because I think he was good, but I agree that Universal should have introduced a new actor in the role. Actually, I remember reading the script some years ago, and when I do this, I cast the film in my mind (as though the film has not yet been made). And, for some reason, I remember envisioning George Reeves in the role of Larry Talbot. I tried to think back to the early 1940s and I recall Reeves in *Gone With the Wind* having the kind of innocence and good looks that would have made him a very sympathetic Talbot. Also, he would have been far more believable as a romantic leading man.

However, my first professional choice would have been to eliminate the entire American background of the character. I have always thought that the background was too contrived and was simply an excuse to cast an American actor in the role (particularly since the reason for the parents' separation is never adequately explained). I would have had Larry be a cultured English gentleman, perhaps on leave from Oxford. He would have been very British, very refined, and this would have made his transformation into a werewolf more shock-ing. As for casting, I saw John Justin in the role. I thought he was great in *The Thief of Bagdad*, particularly in the way he conveyed anguish

Anyway, the magazine is a total delight. Both of your magazines are so professional and attractive that I keep them in my bookcase along with my books. Inciden-

tally, *Cinefantastique* used to be my favorite magazine, but it has since been replaced. Best wishes for continued success.

Nick Anez

Editor's Comments: So true, the contrived plot and casting that made Lon Chaney, Jr. the son of Claude Rains dooms the production from the beginning. The visual juxtaposition of father and son is ridiculous. And I am so glad that people have been coming up with actors of the 1940s era who could have portrayed Larry Talbot in a superior manner. Jack Tydings' letter that follows makes a dandy suggestion.

Dear Gary and Sue:

To your question which actor might have been better suited than Lon Chaney, Jr. to play the Wolf Man in 1941, I couldn't come up with an answer until Sunday.

For what it's worth, here it is. If a casting director were looking for someone to play English aristocracy, someone who was handsome and regal on the one hand yet vulnerable and sympathetic on the other, he might do well to hire Alan Marshall. At the time, Mr. Marshall was a veteran of two noteworthy horror films, *Night Must Fall* (1937) and *The Hunchback of Notre Dame* (1939). He would go on to play a pivotal role in *House on Haunted Hill* (1959). Like Chaney, Jr., of course, he may have been too tall to play the son of Claude Rains, but he could have been photographed in such a manner as to diminish his height.

Jack Tydings

Dear Gary and Sue:

Since 2007 was "the year without a *MidMar*," the arrival of issue #75 was welcome indeed. I thoroughly enjoyed every article, but I have a small nit to pick regarding Gary's opinion that the original *King Kong* "heralded cinematic special effects as both the means and ends of monster cinema." This would probably be a good description of some recent fantasy films, but *King Kong*'s revolutionary (for its time) technology is one of the least important reasons for the film's timeless appeal. Cooper and Schoedsack certainly never thought of stop-frame animation, or any other methods, as the ends, only as the best *means* to put on the screen what would otherwise be un-filmable, or at best look unconvincing.

I usually disagree with Gary's opinions on films, but I think he hit the old nail right on the head with *The Invisible Ray*. Thanks, Gary, for giving this under-appreciated film its due. For some reason, it is often considered the least of the unofficial Karloff-Lugosi trilogy of the mid-1930s, but I consider it the best, for all the reasons Gary specified. One small slip, however. Ronald Drake is the character's name, not the actor. The role was played by Frank Lawton.

I eagerly await issue 76, regardless of which year it is published.

Marc Russell

Editor's Comments: Marc, remember, my heralding of the special effects in *King Kong* was to showcase why it belongs among the top-10 *influential* horror films of all time (and the filmmakers' intentions have nothing to do with the film's ever-increasing influence) and not why it is in itself a cinematic classic. True, the film shines in many ways, but its quantum leap in the quality of special visual effects (thus creating a true performance by Kong) is the prime reason why *King Kong* remains influential, in my estimation.

Dear Gary and Susan:

The publication of *Midnight Marquee* #75 was somewhat delayed, but the finished product was well worth the wait! Virtually every feature this issue is a winner, from Gary J. Svehla's *Groundbreakers* to his 39 pages (!!!) of DVD reviews. The Karloff-Lugosi cover (or is it the Lugosi-Karloff cover?) is a perfect adjunct to Gary D. Rhodes' insightful *Lugosi vs. Karloff—Eternally!* Rhodes chronicles the competitive history between the two monster movie giants, a strange rivalry that has, in the best undead tradition, lived on long after the mortal demise of both men. There is little doubt that Karloff held the upper hand throughout most of their respective careers. Lugosi spent

his final years battling drug addiction and struggling to survive by working for Ed Wood, among others. Karloff, by contrast, spent his twilight decade (the 1960s) hosting and acting in TV's *Thriller*; doing guest shots on shows like *I Spy*, *The Girl from U.N.C.L.E.* and *The Wild, Wild West*; engaging in voice work and TV commercials and acting in such memorable films as *The Raven, Black Sabbath* and *Targets*. By this time Karloff was more beloved than he was menacing, a gentle, avuncular boogeyman figure who was a household name among children and adults alike.

It has been fascinating to watch something of a shift during the past 15 years or so, as interest in Lugosi has grown considerably. Surely Tim Burton's *Ed Wood* (and Martin Landau's Bela Lugosi performance) played a role, and the tragic nature of Lugosi's story probably had an impact as well. Unfortunately a tragic tale is more compelling than a happy one, and the fates seemed to favor Karloff over Lugosi. The prideful Lugosi naturally harbored some professional jealousy toward his counterpart, and now certain fans may feel that "poor Bela" has finally triumphed in the fame game from beyond the grave, posthumously dethroning King Karloff. I don't view it that way, however, and while it is wonderful to see Lugosi receiving some much-deserved attention and acclaim of late, I remain a devoted Karloff follower. Sara Karloff had the right idea when she said some of the classic titles (speaking specifically of *The Bela Lugosi Collection*, where all but one film featured both personalities) should be packaged as collaborations, appealing to fans of *both* stars.

The real winners of the game are the classic horror fans, who have a multitude of choices in this age of DVDs, cable, satellite, HDTV, not to mention modern film and monster magazines, books and websites. Of course there have been technical flaws in some of the DVD releases recounted by Gary Rhodes, and others are woefully lacking in extras or bonus material. Fans should make themselves heard loud and clear, en masse, when such things occur. But this is also a wonderful time to relish the work of both these great perform-ers from the Golden Age of horror. Dracula vs. Frankenstein? Yet what would Dracula be without Lugosi, or Frankenstein's Monster without Karloff or *The Black Cat* with-out either actor? If forced to pick a favorite between cinema's dark duo, I suppose I would choose Karloff for his overall body of work, but at heart I am really a Karloff-Lugosi fan. Or, as they say nowadays, a Lugosi-Karloff fan.

Timothy M. Walters

Editor's Comment: You know Tim, I too have always favored the work of Boris Karloff, but within the past 20 years my appreciation for the talents of Bela Lugosi have escalated. The best of Karloff's work is superior to Lugosi's, but every Lugosi performance mesmerizes and I find I cannot take my eyes off him. Even when acting in Poverty Row productions, Lugosi's perfor-mances always manage to elevate the production to create something interesting. Karloff submitted more cerebral performances; Lugosi's perfor-mances are more visceral and emotional. Dare I use the word fun! But both celebrities are horror film icons, and each individual deserves our appreciation and respect.

Dear Gary:

I hope you and Susan received a great deal of warm appreciation when accepting your Rondo Monster Kid Hall of Fame lifetime achievement award at the recent FANEX. You have been one of the lucky ones: Someone who knew what he wanted to do and did it—and continued doing it, in one form or another, for more than 40 years!

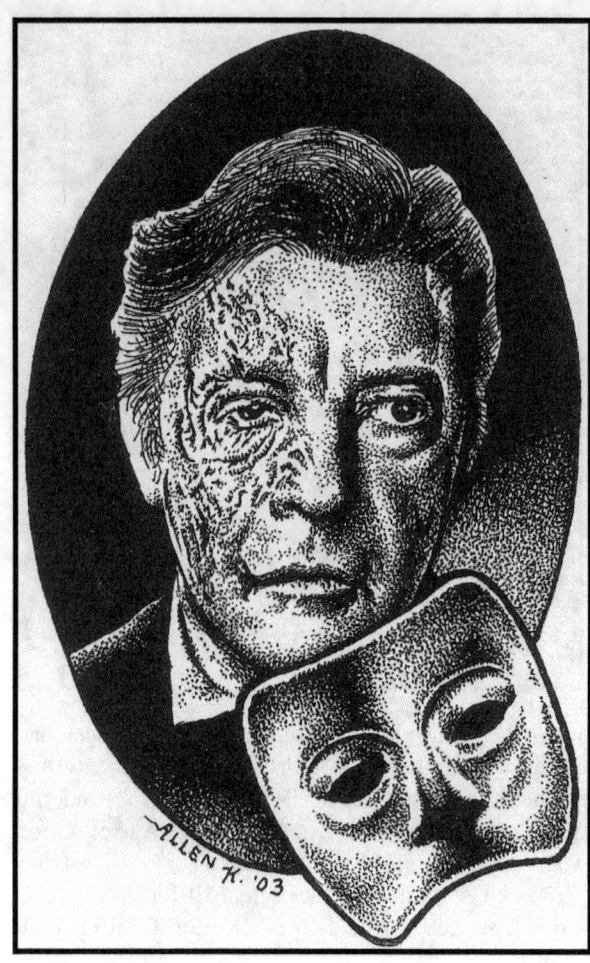

I first encountered *Gore Creatures* in 1968 and faithfully followed it—and now *Midnight Marquee*—ever since, with only a few temporary interruptions. Although as a writer-fan of the genre I "fell by the wayside" in the late 1970s, John Brent (publisher of *Phantasma* and a former student) lured me back. Through John, I learned about FANEX and decided to attend. What I discovered was the live-action, three-dimensional version of the magazine—a chance to re-establish my friendship with Ron Borst and to meet and interact with numerous like-minded people, in many cases people I'd known from a distance through their writings, such as Dick Klemensen, Steve Vertlieb, the late John Parnum, Gary D. Dorst and George Stover.

It was good. It was very good.

And, as a richly decorated bonus, there were the guests, who generally responded to the relaxed and sincere spontaneity of the weekend and who left behind memories of their warmth and humanity, people with the names Carlson, Agar, Harryhausen, Vickers, Leigh and many others.

Through it all, very much a presence was the *pater familias*—Gary Svehla (with Susan).

Congratulations on your award, Gary and Susan. You deserve it. You have made a difference—to me, and to many, many others.

Paul Jensen

Dear Gary Svehla:

Anthony Ambrogio's group editing and collective analyses of *The Wolf Man* (1941) in *MidMar* #75 took me aback, in a happy sense. Might I ask if the same team could do a penetrating textual-photo research uncovering of the scene (lamentably cut from the finished film) where Talbot wrestles the huge bear at the Gypsy carnival. I believe that's Kurt Katch inside the bearskin. The scene does exist in some trailers.

What a great prize this research would be for fandom, the literary complementing the graphic, and both bringing the entire scene to life. Why was the scene edited out by Ted Kent in the first place? This could be potentially fascinating as the discovery of a print of *London After Midnight*.

Marc Vaioli

Editor's Comment: Marc, I can see the merit of a full group discussion on an entire movie (such as the coverage on *Psycho* this issue), but for one brief sequence from one movie, I don't know. Movies of yesterday and today left footage on the cutting room floor, and most of it with good reason. They call it editing, but with today's three-hour movies, the philosophy seems to have fallen by the wayside as directors have far too much

power over the final print (which often is decided by committee, with the filming of several alternate endings becoming the norm). I think such research on the bear wrestling sequence would make a fine sidebar addition to a longer article, but I don't think an entire article, on one deleted scene, would command attention.

Dear Gary and Susan:

Been meaning to write to you for a long time. Just wanted you to know how much I enjoyed your last batch of titles (*Celluloid Adventures, Forgotten Horrors 4, You're Not Old Enough Son and Mantan the Funnyman*). As one of the great comedians of the 1930s and 1940s, Mantan Moreland brought tears to my eyes as I listened to his routines. No matter how many times you're heard them, they still bring on the laughs. I am looking forward to all your new books.

The last four or five months, I went back and reread the back issues of your magazines, as well as a few of the older books. I noticed that when you reprint a title, the new cover seems better than the old one. With your new releases, you must be up to 65 titles or so, though not all of them are still in print (with the exception of two or three books, I have your entire library and very much enjoy browsing through them again and again).

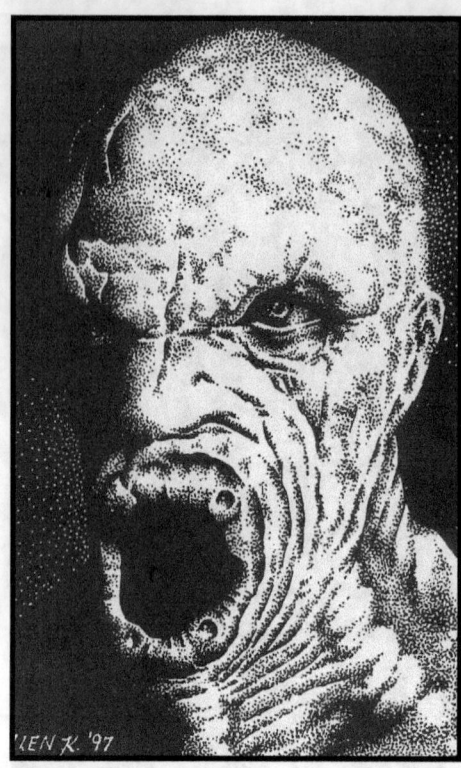

I was using a friend's computer and checked out your website. I was very impressed with all the material you posted for your second feature film, *Terror in the Pharaoh's Tomb*.

I am waiting (with a great deal of impatience) for the next issues of *Mad About Movies* and *Midnight Marquee*. I know the two of you are extremely busy and have your hands in many, many pots. I always love the articles and compare Gary's DVD reviews with my own opinions of the releases.

Hope business is good and improves. Keep up the great work. It's always a pleasure to do business with you, as I get the royal treatment and receive high quality merchandise.

Joseph P. Higgins

Editor's Comments: Joe, people like you keep us going! Sue loves designing covers for our books and magazines, and when we reprint titles, she tries to create an even better cover than before. It makes edition one distinct from the second edition. We even re-edit text, sometimes delete some chapters and add newer ones. So, in a sense, every book is a book-in-progress and each edition is different from the one before. This keeps things fresh and current. It also provides a reason for people to buy the book again. New and improved, in other words.

Dear Gary and Susan:

I am a 56-year-old Hollywood camera-man, living and working in Los Angeles. Gary, I also grew up reading *Famous Monsters of Filmland*, eagerly awaiting the arrival of each issue at my small town drugstore. The articles and photographs in that magazine, *Spacemen* and my personal favorite *Screen Thrills Illustrated*, led me to move from Alabama to L.A. in 1976 for the sole purpose of learning how movies were made. Only days after finding an apartment in seedy Hollywood, I stopped into a local coffee shop, The House of Pies, for breakfast, only to see Forrest J Ackerman doing the same while holding court with fans! What a thrill. To this day, even in frail health, he still manages to visit with fans on Saturdays.

My recent purchase of the book *Forgotten Horrors* led me to your wonderful website (and more books to buy). What a great job you both are doing preserving fading Hollywood history with your books and publications.

I love *Forgotten Horrors* and would like to express my appreciation to Michael H. Price for his great work he has done with the series.

David Riley

Hi Gary and Sue:

The editorial is interesting but I'm one of those people for whom collecting cassettes, laserdiscs, DVDs, Blu-ray DVDs is beyond my budget. To me these terms are just so much magical incantations. Naturally I have picked up a number of films over the years, but I have never been able to build a true collection. I collect books, and that is expensive enough. Your editorial just makes me feel more than ever the outsider to this side of collecting.

I loved your *Groundbreakers* article. As you know I am a sucker for lists. It's hard to fault any of your picks, and you make excellent arguments for them, but here are a few that I would include, and a few that I would remove. I would include *Psycho, Texas Chain Saw Massacre* and the original *Invasion of the Body Snatchers*. I would then remove *Black Sunday, I Was A Teenage Werewolf* and *Ringu*, not because I feel my picks are better films, I love all six of these films, but only because I think my three are perhaps more influential. But it's really hard to disagree with you here.

Lugosi vs. Karloff was an entertaining article concerning a decades-long argument. I love both actors. Both are very interesting people. I can only say that now, at this point in my life, I find Lugosi's work, even the worst of it, more interesting. He somehow makes even the most dismal Poverty Row quickie worth viewing. Karloff (and I love his work) makes acting look effortless, but Lugosi makes it interesting. When they are at the top of their craft (Karloff in *The Body Snatcher*, Lugosi as *Dracula*), they command every scene they grace.

The Wolf Man forum was another fun piece. All the participants made worthy arguments, but in the end I have I say that I swing toward your view. I love *The Wolf Man* as I love all these old Universal monster films (they are old friends that I return to time and time again), but in the end I think it is *Frankenstein Meets the Wolf Man* that really cements the Wolf Man legend. For some reason the first film seems flat to me. In the second film I think Chaney, Jr. (an actor for whom I have a real soft spot, but I couldn't say why) makes the role truly all his own. By the way, writing about *Frankenstein Meets the Wolf Man* and Bela Lugosi earlier brings to mind the one Lugosi role I most dislike — his turn as the Frankenstein Monster. I know his stumbling, shambling portrayal was prompted by the never revealed fact that he was playing the monster as being blind, but it's not really this that bothers me the most. It's his appearance. Lugosi's

face never works for me in that part. He appears too made up, too round. It just looks a little silly to me. Add this to the shambling and you have a creature that just is not very scary for me. Karloff's gaunt features work much better, especially in the first *Frankenstein*. I've often wondered if this may have played a part in the decision to cast Karloff in the original, though I know Lugosi supposedly turned down the role.

I can't comment on everything, but I have a few quick thoughts concerning your DVD reviews. I think we are being too critical nowadays when reviewing a film. Not the general audience, but we the fans, the film buffs. We can analyze and even praise old B programmers from decades ago, but we heap scorn on some of today's honest but flawed efforts. I'm glad to see that you give newer films such as *Boogeyman, The Village, The Ring II, The Exorcist: The Beginning* (though I did see the Schrader version and liked it more), *Land of the Dead* (love the underwater scene) and *Saw* fair assessment. I know all these films have problems, but can't we just go to the movies to have fun anymore? I think we are in a pretty good period for horror films. I saw *30 Days of Night* recently, another flawed film, but it held my interest, had moments of real atmosphere, decent acting and I had a good time.

Maybe I am just mellowing out, as I get older. It doesn't seem too long ago that I was complaining about many of today's horror films. Or is it just that the quality is slowly improving? Who knows! I don't like to analyze too much. It leaches the fun out of these things.

Allen Koszowski

Editor's Comment: Sue would agree with you about critics who ramble on too long with pretentious airs. Of course none of that criticism would be directed toward me, right? The bottom line is that DVDs are expensive, more so with Blu-ray (though amazon.com sells Blu-ray titles for at least 30% off all the time), so people look to the critic to tell him or her the strengths and flaws, not only of the movie itself, but of the package in which it is contained. Besides, many of us haven't seen a specific movie in decades, so the critic is able to remind the viewer how well that title has held up over the years. Besides, good criticism should be informative and stimulating, also fun. That's always been my goal. And let's face facts; most movies of any era are mediocre or worse. Yes, some of today's horror movies deserve merit, but most of them are quick escapist fare (nothing wrong here) that will be forgotten before the month is out. Demographics and marketing have replaced artistic intent.

About your suggestions for influential groundbreaking movies, your suggestion that *Psycho* needs to be added to the list created a flame war that is fully ignited in this very issue. Enjoy the debate!

www.ingramcontent.com/pod-product-compliance
Lightning Source LLC
Chambersburg PA
CBHW05205607O526
44584CB00017B/2212